GHOST TRAILS

Journeys through a lifetime

BY JILL HOMER

For my dad and Geoff,
who both showed me the way

GHOST TRAILS

GHOST TRAILS

GHOST TRAILS

Dalzell Gorge, Alaska
February 27, 2008

I could feel the collapse coming. I could feel it in my heart.

My body shuddered and shook as I knelt into the snow, clutching the frost-coated fabric over my chest in a futile effort to squeeze out the ominous pounding of my pulse. A narrow strip of sky swirled with green light; the rest of the night was so dark I could see flickering reflections across the canyon — a pale, sickly glow. I forced deep breaths and listened against the sinking quiet to the hard beating of my heart. It seemed to think I was sprinting but my mind knew I was barely crawling. If I moved any slower, I'd be dead.

The gnarled silhouettes of spruce trees bent over me like holes cut into the smooth, snow-covered surface of the mountainside. My muscles ached dully as though they had been breaking down slowly for years, and this was the place they were meant to die, like an old Datsun left to rust on some backwoods road. But the nearest road I knew of was 200 miles away. I had pedaled away from that road two days before when I mounted my bicycle and set out toward the deep Alaska wilderness, all in an effort to race to a town some 350 miles distant.

From where I kneeled, the nearest outpost of civilization — a tiny wood-heated cabin and a few tattered tents — was at least 20 miles away. A long way to ride a bicycle — a much longer distance to walk a bicycle, which is what I'd been reduced to, for the past 12 hours, as I waded over a mountain pass blanketed in deep, soft powder. I stood up, coughed violently, and plopped down beside my overturned bicycle, which was weighed down with a lung-busting load of survival gear. My head was spinning. My heart was racing. This was the kind of fatigue that was going to need more than a few minutes of downtime while I caught my breath. This was a full-body revolt.

I sat in the snow and tried to comfort myself with the knowledge that my body was just running low on energy, a condition so common cyclists have bestowed the ugly but appropriate word "bonk" to describe it. But this was unlike any bonk I had ever experienced. It was too comfortable and calm, frighteningly so. Like the last few sputters out of a car engine before it quits, this bonk quietly indicated that there really was nothing left; not for a racer, not for a cyclist, not even for a survivor. I had already spent the last several hours hoping I was at least the last of the three.

"But I am a survivor," I thought angrily. It wasn't like I was actually entirely out of gas. I was still moving and breathing. And I still had a huge tank of fuel strapped to my bicycle. I unzipped my frame bag and fished out a frozen bag of dried cranberries. Using my mittens to chip away at the icy mass, I stuffed handfuls into my mouth and waited for the ice blocks to soften before swallowing.

The carbohydrate clumps felt heavy in my stomach, already lurching with empty nervousness, and I could only force a couple handfuls down before I started to gag. Before I risked losing what I had successfully consumed, I stopped eating.

My dull senses stifled the familiar terror rising from deep corners of my memory. My urge to scream came out as a sigh. A few cranberry calories did not bode well for the ten-hour snow march in front of me. I may or may not survive this, but two things were certain in my mind — I had never been a racer, and I was no longer even a cyclist.

Alone in a remote quadrant of the Alaska Range in late February, my choices were few. I reached for my emergency camping gear on my bicycle, and in the slow-motion struggle of a fly in a refrigerator, I prepared to bed down for a few hours. If I could get a little sleep, could get a little food down, everything would be fine. I could wake up and start pushing again, could march into the human outpost called Rohn, could survive and be alive. My mind was indifferent. My body was less than convinced.

Beside my sleeping bag, the Iditarod Trail was stamped with the footprints of the racers who came before me. Some were large and pocked with stud marks; some were narrow and adorned with the symbols of expensive boot manufacturers. All of them pressed deep into the soft trail. All of them were bordered with the shallow tread of bicycles that had to be pushed, not ridden. All of them had been through this exact same struggle, and all of them had survived — at least to this point.

But rather than feel heartened by the footprints, I felt diminished. Their's was a success story that taunted me in my weakness. They were merely ghosts to me, fading into a future I wanted so badly, disappearing into a distance I needed more than anything.

But I was a just a straggler in this race, trapped in the past — literally trapped — by my own body's inability to move forward. I pressed both mittens into the trail as I shoved my stiffening body toward my bag. My mittens left their own distinctive mark against the footprints, the indelible imprint of bundled fingers and outstretched thumbs, of a human who had been reduced to crawling while others walked. Pretty soon those hand prints would be stamped out by those who followed, the last remaining bicyclists, as well as the runners and the skiers in this race. I smirked in spite of myself at the thought. The race — some race. It was probably one of the few races in the world in which some of its competitors crawled. But was I the only one who was crawling?

The trail was soft and deep now, but eventually the cold would sink in. The trail would set up and harden, only to be blanketed by fresh layers of snow. The racing dog teams would come through and stamp it out again, followed by recreational snowmobiles tracking it out until the warm air of spring left the surface rotten and unusable. Then summer would come and take the rest of the snowpack with it, leaving behind only open tundra and narrow passages through the alder where the trail wound through a canyon below Rainy Pass. In a few short months, there would be no sign of the winter trail or anybody who followed it. The Iditarod Trail was a ghost itself.

But that night, beneath the moonless twilight of the Northern Lights, the Iditarod Trail was more of a ghost than any trail I had followed before. Not in the way it frightened me or battered me, but in the way it haunted me, even as I lay beside it, like it was some distant part of my past and inevitable part of my future.

My journey to that point had been a long one. I had ridden and pushed and pulled my bicycle 200 miles over snow and ice in two days, but even the race was just another leg in my journey. Since the previous November, I had been almost single-mindedly focused on this single race, the 350-mile Iditarod Trail Invitational from Knik to McGrath, Alaska. I had ridden thousands of miles in cold rain and breathtaking wind and snow and ice and sleet, just to prepare for the race. I had spent my downtime poring over maps and reports and ordering gear on the Internet, and working long hours just to pay for it all. But it even went beyond that ... beyond the previous year's human-powered Iditarod race that I followed online like a hopeless fan ... beyond the two 100-mile Alaska snow bike races I had ridden in the two years previous to fulfill my winter lust for adventure ... beyond my decision to move up from the Lower 48 and become a real Alaskan who laughed at winter and scooped up slushy water with my bare hands from holes in the ice. My journey went even beyond that.

But the Iditarod Trail did not care about my history or preparations. It was just a line in the snow. The physical manifestation of the trail had no past or future. The Iditarod Trail was only an idea, written in footprints and tracks, and harbored in the minds of drifters, like myself, who were seeking something along its ever-changing surface.

To those who have never pressed their feet into the Iditarod Trail, the shape of our journey is largely unknown. In a few short days, I had realized our journey at its core is the unknown. What we seek is the truth. Not the truth shaped by human knowledge, but the Truth: harsh, unwritten and startlingly real. There is no ideology that can shield us from the searing wind, the frozen emptiness, the desperate loneliness of a night in the Alaska Range at 20 below. And there are no words that can prepare us for the raw amazement, the sweeping beauty and the quiet joy spread across white, unbroken land. We find so much wonder it makes civilized life seem shallow, and so much pain it makes death seem kind. We find love we can't express in a place so uncaring it breaks our hearts. We find that we're stronger than we ever hoped to be and weaker than we ever imagined. We find that there is reason to hope, and there is always reason to hope, as long as weary hearts keep beating. And what we realize is that everything we were looking for was inside of us, all along.

I took one last glance at the twisting spruce shadows before I zipped up my bag and closed out the green-tinted night. My shallow, frightened breaths finally began to slow as the body-heated humidity of my sleeping bag surrounded me. I switched off my headlamp and pulled my icy bladder of drinking water next to my torso, wincing as the chill of my ice baby cut through to my heart. Despite my pounding pulse and churning stomach, I could feel my muscles relax and eyelids droop. A curtain of warmth settled over my thoughts and I closed my eyes. I could feel my fear melting into the serene indifference of sleep. I wondered if I would ever wake up. I had no way of knowing for sure.

Bells Canyon, Utah
Summer 1990

The year after the Berlin Wall fell, Becky and I no longer felt reason to fear. So we reinvented ourselves as adventurers.

Before that we were sixth graders, pulling our stringy hair back in ponytails and combing the suburbs in search of identities. We spent the summer traversing sidewalks, kicking the cuffs of manicured lawns and plotting our routes by a progression of whimsical mailboxes.

"There's the fish with the big mouth," Becky said. "My Dad has something like that hanging in the garage. His one sings."

While we were busy daydreaming aloud about Arctic expeditions and our futures in professional photography and novel writing, the wide-mouthed mailbox fish always alerted us back to our place in the world. We were two blocks from the red barn, three more to the windmill, and the next blue mailbox marked Becky's house.

It was easy to feel powerful when we were walking. We were out on our own, out where our parents couldn't tell us to wash the dishes and teachers couldn't ask us to use "attractive" in a sentence and the popular girls couldn't laugh shrilly at unheard jokes we suspected were directed at us. School and home were wildernesses of confusing expectations that neither of us felt that comfortable navigating. Becky struggled with her grades and was always getting sick and missing school. I sucked at sports and dance and gymnastics, and I couldn't wedge myself into my preferred social circles. But when we went outside, those distinctions didn't matter. We could talk about school like it was a silly game and giggle at our own inside jokes like the girls at recess and wave at the older boys playing basketball at the park. When we were mobile, the thrill of new experience moved with us — there was never a chance for it to settle, to become stale, to decay.

It was with this fresh outlook that we discovered Becky's dad's coffee table book about Mount Denali, splashed with colorful pictures and stowed away on a dusty bookshelf in the front room. I saw distant mountains outside my bedroom window every day, but never anything like the mountains in that book — jagged, whitewashed and hovering above a ceiling of clouds that I could only imagine meant they were the roof of the world.

The photos were alternately stark and fuzzy. In some, climbers squinted in the sunlight and cast unassuming smiles at the camera. In others, lines of climbers hunched in blizzards so complete it looked like their blurry images had been cut out and pasted on a piece of white paper. Then there were the photographs in which climbers sat in tents with purple blisters on their cheeks and glassy-eyed, distant looks on their faces. Those vacant gazes were as intriguing as the moonscapes where they walked.

"What are those purple marks?" I asked Becky.

She scanned the photo captions. "Frostbite," she answered.

The summer burned hot and frostbite was thousands of miles away. But where we walked, the abstraction of adventure was beginning to take shape. The pictures of Denali lingered in our thoughts, and instead of watching for the big-mouth fish, we began to avert our gaze to the eastern mountains. Knife-edged granite peaks carved a stark silhouette against the sky. Streaks of snow still lined the high peaks even as we roasted in 90-degree afternoons in the valley. The mountains were so close we could almost reach out and touch them, but so far they still clung to remnants of winter in July.

"Does your family ever take you hiking?" I asked Becky.

"Yeah, all the time," she said. "We went to Bells Canyon last month. I think that's it." She gestured at a narrow depression cut into a nearby slope. "It's kinda steep, but it's really pretty up there. There's a waterfall, and this meadow with wildflowers."

"Wow, it sounds really cool," I said. "So you know where the trail is?"

"Yeah. Just off Wasatch Boulevard."

"Do you think your parents would let us go hiking in Bells Canyon?" I knew my mom would disapprove, but Becky's dad was all about trial-by-fire adventure for all of his children. He would probably even drive us to the trail head. I could tell my mom I was going for a walk with Becky, and that's all she needed to know.

"That'd be fun," Becky said. She stopped walking and directed all of her focus toward her new role as mountain guide. "Let's see. We'll need water, and some granola bars. You'll need a backpack to borrow. I think my brother's old one is still in the closet. How comfortable are those shoes?"

After much coaxing, Becky's older brother agreed to drive us to the trail head and pick us up in two hours.

"I'm going to be back at 4, so don't be late. I'll leave your butts here, I swear I will."

And with that, we were standing alone at a wooden sign with the words "Bells Canyon" painted in yellow. A sun-faded map behind some glass plotted the trail. It might as well have been Sanskrit. We studied it briefly before hoisting our granola-bar-filled bookbags and stepping onto the dirt.

The trail ascended quickly and my lungs burned amid clouds of dust being swept off the foothills by a stiff breeze. I looked around for a view of the snow-capped peaks, but all I could see was skeletal scrub oak with tiny leaves that offered little shade. Becky and I breathed deep, uncharacteristically wordless, concentrating our thoughts into motion rather than the other way around. Becky was taller and faster than I was, and after several minutes I could no longer see her ahead of me. Alone, I clawed my way up the hillside, coughing dust and wiping grimy sweat from my forehead. My bookbag rested against a puddle of sweat on my back.

"What's wrong with this trail?" I thought. "This isn't fun." I tried to call out to Becky, to tell her to wait up, to talk her into turning around, but she was out of range.

When I didn't catch up to her at a stream crossing, a dark cloud of dread descended over me. The roar of the water rang in my ears as I walked up to the bank. The water boiled white as it swept beneath a bundle of pine tree logs. With branches and needles still attached, they appeared to be the only bridge. I couldn't believe anyone in the history of the world had crossed this torrent, let alone Becky, but she was nowhere to be seen. I paced back and forth, calling her name. I could barely hear my own words over the rushing water.

That was it. Becky was dead, and I was going to have to be the one to tell her family. The thought seemed ridiculous, but at the same time, too plausible for comfort. Anyway, if she wasn't dead, I couldn't be the one to just leave her there.

I knelt at the log at placed both hands on the wet bark. Then I grabbed a sappy branch and crawled onto the largest log, crouching like a frog as I crept forward. I couldn't help but look down. I felt like I could only look down as I inched over the open water, which was boiling and churning so wildly that all I could see was white, stark white, a whiteout as complete as any moonscape or blizzard.

When I reached the other side I began to run up the trail, desperate to find Becky because I still couldn't quite believe she hadn't fallen into the water. I began to breathe hard and felt my lungs burning. I was breathing fire, but I couldn't stop running.

"Becky! Becky," I wheezed, until my desperate breaths stole my voice. Seasons passed. White spots began to cloud my vision. I ran until I tripped and fell to my hands and knees. I was hunched over on the trail, gasping for air, when Becky jogged back toward me.

"Where have you been?" she asked. "I waited for you up there, but, oh, we're not going to have time to make it to the waterfall. We have to get back before my brother comes. Why are you going so slow?"

I just wheezed and gulped and shook my head. "Well, come on," Becky said. "Let's go back."

I followed Becky back to the log bridge, certain that I was incapable of crossing it again, but hoping that if I could only watch her do it, I'd be OK. She stepped onto the narrow crossing, held out her arms, and walked across it. Walked with perfect confidence, as though she were an Olympic gymnast on a balance beam. Just four steps and she was done. I stood my ground on the wrong side, still wheezing, bewildered. If ever in my life I had been doomed, it was then.

"Are you coming?" she shouted over the rapids.

I shook my head. "I can't," I said, speaking barely above a whisper.

"What?" she yelled.

"I can't!" I yelled back more forcefully. As far as I could tell, truer words had never been spoken.

Becky was going to have to go home and summon a helicopter. That's all there was to it. A look of concern washed briefly across Becky's face, and then she grimaced.

"You have to!" she shouted. "Just walk across it; it's not hard." I shook my head. She began to walk upstream and stopped at the deepest, loudest stretch of the channel. "Well, try jumping then," she said. "Right here. It's pretty close here."

I walked over to Becky's channel and stared into the churning whiteout. It was a gorge, a chasm. It didn't matter that it was only about three feet across. It was a universe.

"Go back a ways," Becky instructed me. "Run, and then jump."

Fear and anger boiled in my gut. As a 10-year-old, it was my job to stay home and watch after-school cartoons and learn my long division. It was not my job to leap over the stream of death. The ugly landscape of scrub oak and dust and barren mountainsides swirled all around me. I felt dizzy. I couldn't focus. A blizzard of white light shot through my field of vision. The sweat on my forehead cooled and trickled down my face like melted ice. I walked back to the edge of the trees, turned around, and launched into a dead sprint straight at Becky. I thought I could see her cheering me on as my last foot left the ground and I clawed at the sky, the churning water so close I could feel frigid droplets hit my legs as I flew through the air. Then I was on the ground again, a heap in the dust.

"Wow, nice jump," Becky said. But she looked nervous and coaxed me to get up quickly. As I brushed myself off, I noticed there was a little blood on one of my knees.

Becky was already hiking down the trail again. As I followed her down the trail at a slight limp, tears started to trickle down my face. I did not fight them, and I didn't try to chase her. Surviving the jump did not make me feel happy. It made me feel even more helpless and scared. I couldn't blame Becky because the hike was my idea. I couldn't keep up with her because my knee hurt. She wouldn't wait for me because she actually thought her brother was going to leave us, even though he really never would. It all seemed so cruel, cruel enough to cancel out all the beauty of the mountains, cruel enough to be pointless.

The trail, so distinct when I had followed it up, began to fade. Matted grass covered the surface, until I reached an open meadow and couldn't see a trail at all. I pushed into the brush and groped around for an opening. Maybe I had taken a wrong turn. Where their wrong turns on this trail?

I turned back toward the scrub oak and tried to retrace my path. I finally located hints of the thin dusty line on the other side of a wall of vegetation. I pushed through tall strands of pale green plants, when suddenly my arms and neck erupted in a blast of fire. I yelped with pain and leapt backward, clutching both arms with both hands as red welts boiled up on my skin. Stinging nettle.

I had never seen it before, nor did I know what it was at the time. All I knew was I was being attacked. Everything about Bells Canyon, about the mountains, was lashing out against me, and all I had wanted to do was go for a hike.

Knik, Alaska
February 24, 2008

"You in that bike race?" a man on a bar stool asked as I stomped across mud-caked linoleum in my expedition winter boots.

"Who me?" I replied, and nodded. "Yes, I am."

"So what's a girl like you doing in a race like that?"

The Knik Bar, dark and dingy at midday, was a flurry of incompatible activity. Men in oil-stained Carhartt jackets and shiny snowmobile suits crowded around the counter, filling half the building with traditional Alaskan values and amused facial expressions. On the other side of the bar, which was set up restaurant style, were table after table of Europeans in down jackets and ski boots, skinny cyclists in knee-high overboots and lycra-clad runners wearing sneakers when it was 20 degrees outside. The athletes devoured big plates of hamburgers and didn't seem to notice me at all, but the real Alaskans swilling beer and whiskey at 1 p.m. made known their disapproval.

"Sorry?" I said, slowing my bee-line for the bathroom and removing my sunglasses to reveal skin already flushed after mere minutes in the February sun. The man wore a brown knit hat and a flannel shirt. He was squinting in a thin stream of light that had escaped through a crack in the front door.

"You're with those people, right?" he asked, nodding to the other side of the bar.

"Yes," I said, glancing at the large group that looked as obviously out of place as tuxedos and evening gowns at a barn dance. I had never met a single one of them.

"And you're gonna be in that race? That Iditabike?"

"Yes," I said.

Brown hat laughed. "You're crazy. All of you. Crazy."

"Yeah," I said. "I get that often."

"If my daughter wanted to do that, ride a bike across the tundra," the man said as he nudged another guy sitting next to him, "I'd kill her. I would. It would be a less painful way to die." His friend laughed. He was almost a mirror image of brown hat, but with stubble on his chin, and a blue parka.

"Did you bring a gun?" the man in the blue parka said.

"Um, no," I said.

"Gotta have a gun," he said. "There's moose out there. A lot of em. They'll stomp you just as soon as look at you."

"Right," I said, looking around for the best way to make my exit for the bathroom.

"People think bears are the thing to be afraid of; they think in the winter they're safe," blue parka continued. "But that ain't how it goes. Moose are the most dangerous animal around. More deaths than by bear every year."

"Ah, she don't need to worry too much about moose," brown hat said. "She needs to worry about bad ice."

"Bad ice," blue parka nodded. "Gets a lot of snowmachiners. I heard the Yentna froze uneven again this year. And then we got that rain last week."

Brown hat laughed. "Rain? Can you believe it?"

"I heard," I said.

"But you're not from around here?" brown hat said. I shook my head. "None of them are, either. You all come a long way for this Iditabike. Most Outsiders aren't prepared for what Alaska's really like."

"I'm from Juneau," I said.

Brown hat and blue parka just smiled.

"I should go," I said, and without waiting for a goodbye or more advice from real Alaskans, walked quickly into the empty ladies' room.

Outside, the blue sky blazed clear and cold, wrapped like a blanket around a heatless sun. It was an affront to my Juneau sensibilities, which had been softened by gray skies and endless days of cool rain.

Even at its most harsh, Juneau is tropical compared to the deep-frozen desert of Interior Alaska. North of the Alaska range, where ocean breezes never blow, temperatures whip around like a condemned carnival ride. It could be 40 degrees or minus 40 degrees; neither is very livable. Winds blow at hurricane force, driving chills to flash-freezing depths. And they bring storms, raging storms, storms that will erase the whole world, fill it with blinding snow and lock a woebegone traveler in a frantic state of motionlessness — like static on a television screen. Juneau is not the place to live if one is trying to prepare oneself for what Alaska's really like.

I stopped to check my pockets, confirming I still had sunglasses, sunscreen, a GPS and my fleece gloves. Two Clif Bars rested against my ribs, borrowing body heat to keep them from freezing into inedible blocks. I pulled on my fleece hat and unzipped my own winter shell to make sure all the layers were there — fleece pullover, vapor barrier vest, polypro base layer. Beneath soft-shell pants and polar tights, my knee braces and cycling shorts squeezed my skin. I had gators, wool socks, vapor barrier socks, nylon socks and a headband to pull over my nose if my face started to get cold.

The clothing hugged my body like a scuba suit, but I couldn't have felt more naked as I stood in the snow-packed parking lot between lines of snowmobiles and gear-laden bicycles. The glaring sun was about to expose me for the fraud I was. I wasn't an athlete like the down-bundled Euros, and I wasn't a real Alaskan like the owners of those snowmobiles. The men at the Knik Bar had said it all between a couple swigs of beer. A girl like me didn't belong in a race like this.

I shuffled over to my bike and grunted as I hoisted it out of a snow bank. It was loaded down with a bunch of gear I had technically never tested, and I had no idea how much it weighed. My most optimistic guess was 65 pounds. It could have easily been 10 more ... either way, more than half my own body weight. The bike itself was weighted with bags that contained a bunch of stuff I had only used in theory, while camping in my back yard or very near by: a sleeping bag rated to 40 below zero, a bivouac sack, a foam pad, extra clothing, stove, lighter, bike repair kit, medical kit, drugs, food, water.

The list weighed heavily in my mind. This was my survival gear. My survival gear. I wasn't just going out for a fun overnight camping jaunt. I was pedaling into deep Alaska backcountry in February with no one to depend on but myself, and I somehow had to live through it. It suddenly struck me just how imbalanced my training had been. I had spent 25 hours some weeks putting in hard miles, riding for 10 hours straight, lifting weights, running intervals, trekking through soft snow. In those same weeks, I'd spend maybe one hour total browsing the Internet for the cheapest used sleeping bag I could find, testing my stove in the back yard, compiling a vague food list.

How could I have been so nonchalant about my preparation? Why did I waste so much time on fitness? In a race like this, the biking's actually optional. The survival stuff's not.

I wheeled my bike over to Geoff, my boyfriend and fellow competitor, who was fiddling with some of the straps on his sled. Geoff entered the race in the foot division. In our two and a half years in Alaska together, he had emerged as an accomplished ultra-runner, dominating local races and blowing up records as a relative novice. He was a real athletic force compared to my weekend warrior, "everyone's a winner if they have fun" persona. But we had both entered a race that took participants 350 human-powered miles over the Iditarod Trail, something only a few hundred people in history had ever signed up to do. I was one of a few dozen women to ever take on the challenge. Among the 650,000 other Alaskans who were driving in cars, watching TV and shopping for new carpet, there were a few who were willing to give us credit as the state's hardcore elite. But certainly not anyone in the Carhartt half of the Knik Bar.

The Iditarod Trail Invitational, the current human-powered version of the much more famous Iditarod Sled Dog Race, had flown under the radar for so long that it had morphed into something of an urban legend. "Bikes on snow?" my coworkers had said. "I've heard about that. People don't really do that, do they?" There's no money in racing it and even less glory. You're more likely to be branded crazy than strong. You'll be called stupid by more people than would ever call you brave.

So why bother entering it? And if you're not a really strong cyclist, why enter it? And if you're a scared little desert-bred girl from the Mormon suburbs of Salt Lake City, why enter it? I had asked it myself so many times that the question became its own answer, like the famous cop-out first uttered by doomed Everest mountaineer George Mallory. I entered it to enter it. Because it was there.

Bill Merchant, the wiry, 50-something race director and longtime participant, had a more eloquent idea.

"This trail gets under your skin, gets into you," he said to me while we spoke briefly before the start of the race. "People keep coming back year after year. They don't know why."

"Because it's fun?" I offered weakly.

"Oh yeah, it's fun."

"Or because they forget it's awful?"

"That too."

Bill waved me over to the starting line. I leaned over to share a last, lingering hug with Geoff. We had known each other more than seven years; we had always been partners in each others' adventures, cheerleaders for each others' goals. None of that factored into our thoughts the moment we let go. We were here to run our own race. This was my adventure in self-sufficiency. His adventure in solitude. We broke away from our embrace. I nodded and took my position next to the cyclists. The last time I glanced over, he was looking forward down the trail. The chasm I felt between him and me was as deep as a divorce. We assumed our roles as competitors in the biggest race of our lives, staring into a playing field as long as Alaska itself.

The clock crept closer to 2 p.m., Sunday, Feb. 24, 2008. The tyranny of my gear list crept back into my head. What had I forgotten? What had I brought? I stood side by side with strangers. Some were the endurance cycling elite, heroes who I would see for these anxious few seconds and then likely would never cross paths with again as we spread out over 350 miles of terrain. A giant sign that read "Alaska Ultrasport" marked the beginning of the trail, which followed waves of frozen snowmobile tracks over the surface of Knik Lake.

Less than a half mile from the start, the trail shot up a steep embankment and disappeared into the woods. I fixated on its vanishing point. Spindly spruce trees guarded it like a fortress, dark and jagged against a solid blue sky. I had no idea where the trail went beyond those trees. No idea at all. Would I even be able to find it?

Every planned experience has its moment when expectations meet reality, and often they don't connect. This was my moment, the moment I became acutely aware of my own smallness and inadequacy. Uncertainty flooded my gut with bricks and bile. I wanted to lean over and vomit, and had to fight the urge to do so. What did I have left to purge? What part of me thought I had the stomach for this race? Or the heart?

All of the insecurities I had been coddling during my short two hours in Knik flooded to the surface. I was the two-year resident of southern Alaska, the one who had never seen a temperature below minus 15 and never ventured more than 25 miles from a road. I was the cyclist who once struggled through 50 miles a day of a relaxed road tour. I was the hiker who had a panic attack on Mount Borah because I saw a few snow flurries. I was the teenager who cultivated an interest in the outdoors mainly because it garnered cool points with cool boys. I was the scared little girl who got lost during a mile-long hike on a major trail.

I did not belong there.

I did not hear anyone say "go."

East Canyon, Utah
April 19, 1996

"Are we really headed up there now?" John asked as he turned the steering wheel and merged onto Interstate 80.

"What are you talking about?" Spencer asked. "We're already nearly there."

"It is ..." John paused while he squinted at the flickering display on a geriatric car stereo. "It's 6 o'clock. So, yeah, we only have ... what ... 12 hours to kill in a parking lot?"

"Thirteen," Spencer said. "The ticket counter opens at 7."

"Do we really need to get there this early? I mean, really, who's going to be standing in line 13 hours ahead of time?"

"We're talking about Tori Amos," Spencer said with mock offense. "Who wouldn't?"

From my position in the back seat, with my head pressed against a fogged window, it was hard to comprehend what a Tori Amos concert could mean to the world at large versus what it meant to my 16-year-old values. Everything I needed was in that car, in that canyon — friends, freedom, the promise of adventure and something to hope for in the future. And there was Spencer, who was sitting right next to me with the prospect that he'd stay that way all night. Spencer, who I hadn't yet dared to look directly in the eyes for fear he'd look away.

The sun rolled low on the horizon behind us as we drove into the shadows of

Parley's Canyon. The green wash of new growth that coated the Salt Lake Valley in April was already beginning to fade. Broad leaves changed to tiny buds, which changed to bare branches as the elevation climbed, and further up drifts of dirty snow clung to the mountainside. I was fascinated with the barren landscape, moving further into winter as though we were moving back in time.

"It's going to be cold tonight," Jenny spoke up in from the passenger seat. "Did we bring any blankets?"

"Spencer grabbed some sleeping bags. We should be good," John said as his battered boat of a Buick started to sputter on the steepening grade. "I mean, we'll be good if we don't have to spend 13 hours huddled in sleeping bags in an empty parking lot."

"OK, then, let's do something," Spencer said. "Let's go for a hike or something."

"I don't know," Jenny said. "I think we should try to get there as early as possible."

"Trust me, Jenny, no one else is going to be lining up to spend all night in front of an Albertsons in Park City," John said. It's going to be boring and frozen. Nope, we're going to be the only dumbasses out there until dawn. I'd put money on it."

The rhetorical bet made me smile. I would have paid a million dollars to be where I was. I couldn't believe the rest of the world wasn't willing to join me.

"There's something," Spencer said, looking in the direction of a sign marking an exit. It simply read "East Canyon. No Services."

"East Canyon," Spencer said. "I feel like I've been there before. We could check out the canyon. That'd kill some time right there."

"East Canyon it is," John said, banking the car wide over the rumble strips as we jolted off the interstate and onto unmarked gravel. John crossed beneath the highway and started up a wide canyon. The Buick had only been bouncing down the road for five minutes when Spencer leaned into the front seat.

"Right there," Spencer said. "Stop there."

"What? Where?" John looked over his shoulder.

"Ahead," Spencer said. "Right there. Hike. There."

"What are you talking about? I don't see anything. I see a pullout. Spencer, that's not a hiking trail."

"Good as any," Spencer said. "We park here. We hike there." He pointed up a steep slope, choked with scraggly sagebrush and cut by a single narrow channel of loose scree. "Up. Hike. There. We'll go up and see what we can see."

"Whatever," John said as he pulled the car to a stop. "I told you we should have stayed home and headed out in the morning. I even rented 'Labyrinth.'"

"Damn, it's cold out here," Jenny yelled as she stood out of the car with one foot still planted inside. I jiggled my own door open and stepped out into the chilled air. A blast of wind sliced like needles through my T-shirt, which was oversized and black with a big Smashing Pumpkins-trademark "ZERO" screen printed on the front. As far as I was concerned, it was the most attractive shirt I had, but it did nothing to barricade the cutting cold. Spencer all but sprinted out of the car and bounded up the hillside in his faded Army jacket and holey jeans with stick figures scribbled in ball-point pen across the thighs. His long blond hair whipped like a frayed flag in the breeze. I held my own hair back with my hand. Jenny and John held the car doors open with bewildered looks on their faces.

"Really?" John called out.

Spencer took a few more sliding steps up the scree and turned around. "C'mon, it's a beautiful evening," he yelled. He took a deep breath and began to sing in his best falsetto, "The Hi-il-il-ills are aliiiiiive."

I walked toward him, trying to cast my own smile as bemused while hiding the fact that I was secretly deeply impressed. As long as I had known him, about six months, Spencer was perpetually sidetracked into something theatrical. I could never tell what he was passionate about and what he was mocking. His signals were impossible to read and I began to take from them what I wanted, what I thought I needed them to be. His take-no-excuses assault of a nameless hillside told me was gunning for a way to separate the couples, Jenny and John, him and me, and I was determined to keep up with that moment.

His "Sound of Music" impressions faded out pretty quickly as we fought our way up the gravely hillside. We'd take two steps forward, and slide three steps back, stopping to rest only to feel the wind bite deeper as it brushed our sweat-soaked backs. John, trudging several steps ahead of me, seemed resigned to the prison sentence of the whole night. Jenny, just behind me, grumbled audibly until still finally announced her intention to wait for us at the car, and started back down.

Spencer, silent up front, didn't stop, and John marched like a wounded bear between us. There was no way around him.

The scree-filled channel faded out and we were soon traversing an open, grassy hillside. It wasn't as steep, but there was no evidence we were anywhere near an overlook. I glanced around nervously as I felt myself losing track of the scree trail. Now we were just weaving through open terrain. I had no idea where we were going; I only knew I was following Spencer to the frigid end. Wherever that may be.

I wanted John to go back and find Jenny. I wanted Spencer to turn around and tell me he had invited me to come with him to get tickets tonight because he really wanted to go to the concert with me and spend more time hanging out with me. I wanted Spencer to tell me that I wasn't just another arrow in his quiver of friends and music and thrift store clothing, which he was always shooting into the sky as he conquered his way to a cool existence. I wanted to be the conquest. I wanted to be the existence. I wanted to know where I was.

Spencer veered away from the uphill climb and began to walk laterally along the slope.

"Uh, isn't the top up there?" John asked.

"I think the view will be better this way," Spencer said, pointing to an edge on the hill that seemed to dip downward. I imagined a beautiful vista just over its horizon line, but when we reached the point, all there was to see was more sagebrush, more grass, more hill. And Spencer kept going, moving almost downhill now, still away from our original path.

On every hike I'd ever been on, there'd always been evidence of steps that came before. I never realized how much comfort could be derived from stacks of sandstone piled on top of larger boulders, letters slashed into bark or shoeprints in the mud. Trail-blazing was different. There was no sense that a path was right and good because it had been picked by somebody else. There was only the wilderness — unbroken, unmarked and unmapped as far as we were concerned. Did it even have anything to offer us? Any kind of real destination? Spencer didn't seem to care. Without direction we were free to wander. And it was the wandering, not the destination, that mattered.

We hit a wall of sagebrush and Spencer took another sharp left. I looked for a way to weave ahead of John but the brush held me to our narrow path. Spencer was humming something that I couldn't quite hear. There was no longer a view of either the road or the car. The wind needled through my clothing and chilled beads of sweat on the back of my neck. I gasped with each big gust. The cold had entered my bloodstream; it was surrounding my heart. There was a foreboding feeling of real danger but I couldn't let Spencer see me shiver. I couldn't tell him I felt lost.

"Where are you going?" John said.

"Um, back toward the car," Spencer said, as though John should have known that all along.

"No overlook?" I asked, stifling an urge to chatter my teeth.

"It's not like we had time to walk all the way up a mountain," Spencer said. "We're just out getting some fresh spring air."

"Yeah, taste that spring air," John wheezed, his voice going sour amid the wind and walking. "Spence, I'm about to morph into a popsicle. Can we please hurry?"

"Yeah, yeah, yeah, quit yer whining. We're going back." Spencer turned and smiled. His teeth were huge, and they glowed pale orange in the fading sunlight. I tried to remember the first time I had seen his smile ... when I brushed by him and his friends at the thrift store? When my best friend and I conveniently bumped into him at one of his high school's football games? Over the phone when he first called me out of the blue? I thought often about the first time he called me.

Even though I couldn't see him at the time, I felt his smile, in my gut, as though it were approaching me at a dead sprint before we launched off a mountain together.

Then it was months of not much, before his random call the night before: "Hey, you're into Tori Amos, aren't you? Well, me and my friends are headed up to Park City to be the first in line to buy concert tickets ..."

I held my breath until he asked me if I wanted to go with him. How do you tell someone you'd follow them off a mountain? ... "Yeah, Tori Amos is pretty cool," I had said nonchalantly over the phone. "What time are you guys leaving?"

Even as I felt surrounded by cold and growing fear, Spencer seemed more loose and comfortable with every step. I couldn't drum up the courage to tell Spencer how I felt about him. I couldn't even hike well enough to walk with him on the hillside. There was never anything tangible to hold me back — no real trail, no real barriers. There was only the vague sense that he did not feel the same way. It was a wall higher than any vertical cliff in the world.

We started dropping steeply down the hillside when we reached the original gravel wash that we had climbed up. "Oh look," Spencer said, waving his arms back and forth and mimicking his best Grover-from-Sesame-Street impression. "It's the car."

I looked down and sure enough, there was the roof of the car several dozen feet below us. I could even see Jenny's sullen face through the windshield. Spencer jumped into the loose pebbles, held out his arms and took long, loping strides down the slope. John and I tentatively entered his path and side-stepped down the scree, wavering and biting our lips as we struggled to keep our balance. As we carefully moved downward, flecks of white began to flutter in front of our faces.

By the time we reached the safety of flat ground, the flurries gave way to a full storm. Swirling snow fell from a single dark cloud that hung over a lavender sky, still framed in orange sunlight.

"Oh, this is great," John said as he walked to the car and jerked open the driver-side door, brushing snowflakes from his hair. "Just what we need right now."

By then Spencer didn't hear him because he had already sprinted several dozen feet down the road. He was twirling and laughing, a silhouetted figure backlit by sunset colors and surrounded in the novelty of a spring blizzard.

"It's snowing! It's snowing!" Spencer sang. His voice echoed as the snow-speckled air distorted his dancing silhouette like a flicker of abstract shapes. I felt a sting of sadness, because I knew I was never going to love him more than I did right then.

Yentna River, Alaska
February 24, 2008

There was little time to get lost in the crowd.

In the fury of the race start, the small peloton fanned out over the frozen surface of Knik Lake and broke apart within seconds. Cyclists laid into their pedals and skiers made long, sweeping strokes.

The foot competitors — who in any other race would be called runners, but in a multiday race like the Iditarod Trail Invitational are generally referred to as walkers — actually ran, loping across the lake like they intended to keep that pace for 350 miles.

The strongmen among the cyclists took a sharp left toward a legal shortcut, which the inexperienced, myself included, didn't dare attempt for fear of being dropped.

Both of my ice cleats fell off my feet within 100 yards of the starting line. I stopped to pick them up before standing out of the saddle just to crank up the first hill. My refusal to take the shortcut and my short stop put me solidly behind all but a few straggling cyclists but in front of every walker and skier. And there, just a half mile from the starting line, I had unknowingly established my status for the rest the race.

The afternoon sun soaked in as I gave up the pointless starting-line sprint and settled into a sustainable pace — "sustainable" only meaning I had tested that pace in a handful of 10-hour training rides that I, until that moment, thought were really tough. But I was 20 minutes into the real deal and already sucking wind. As sweat boiled up from my "minimum" clothing layers — which I had no other space to store but on my own body — I began to rethink everything, again.

Had I actually overpacked? Undertrained? My heart was racing and my legs protested under what I thought was a routine effort. I stole a quick glance at my GPS receiver. I had traveled four miles.

"Settle down, settle down," I told myself, wishing I had taken the time to establish some kind of mantra that didn't sound like a mother scolding her unruly toddler. "Take it easy. Sit back. This is a long race. A long race. A long, long race." The mantra began to sink in. "Long race," I chanted again. Long race meant there was no foreseeable end to the suffering, so I might as well get used to it.

Still, I noticed that my wheels were rolling surprisingly easy. In all of the anxiety and frenzy of the race start, I had failed to notice what amazing shape the trail was in.

In any kind of snow cycling, the condition of the trail is the largest unknown and generally makes the largest difference. Weather, terrain, gear, food, fitness, skill, climbing, descending — everything takes a back seat to the nature of The Trail. Forged over an ever-changing surface, snow trail conditions can mean the difference between a laborious, 1.5 mph slog through frozen sugar and an effortless 15 mph sprint over hard ice. In any given year, the Iditarod Trail doles out plenty of unworkable situations, which can shift by the hour and even the minute. Those who finish the race are those who cope best with this reality. Those who finish the race are those who ride strong but do not give up hope while they crawl.

But this year, at mile five of an unfathomable 350, the Iditarod Trail was hard-packed and smooth. Fat, four-inch-wide tires on top of any kind of surface don't exactly roll easy, but I was becoming more and more comfortable with 10 mph — for me, an almost unthinkably fast pace. The fast movement soothed some of my apprehension, and I began to glance around at my surroundings.

Spindly spruce trees cast shadows over the rolling hills as skeletal alder branches and frost-coated cow parsnip stalks poked out of the thick snow cover. There is a sameness to Alaska's winter terrain as it crawls up river valleys and approaches mountains. It's a sameness that becomes even more pronounced as it dips into the deeply frozen Interior, where every form of life struggles to survive. Despite the extreme climate, the spruce and alder remain. Even as they become scrawnier and sparser with every mile, they remain. Even as they're nearly devoured by frozen swamps as pristinely blank as the surface of the moon, they remain. There's a quiet beauty to that staying power, a consistency I take comfort in even as the sameness begins to tug at my sanity.

As the evening sun began to sink into the horizon, I rolled across Flathorn Lake. The landscape felt as familiar and friendly as a route I had ridden a hundred times, but I had only been to that spot twice in my life. In the two years prior, I entered a race called the Susitna 100, a 100-mile event that looped around this part of the Iditarod Trail.

What compelled me to enter my first Susitna 100 is something I'll never fully understand. It was early winter in 2005. I was a brand new Alaskan, having motored up the Alaska Highway just months before. I was a recreational bicycle tourist, a lapsed one at that, with only a marginal interest in mountain biking. I had never competed in a race in my adult life — cycling, running, charity event or otherwise. It was Thanksgiving break — a brutally cold, blizzard-filled Thanksgiving break — when I grabbed a Susitna 100 brochure at the Anchorage REI.

"Bikes on snow!" I told Geoff. "That could be fun."

"Or crazy," Geoff replied. And that was all. Such a meaningless moment. A brochure. A few pithy comments. But I kept that brochure in my car and eventually looked up the race Web site. That was all it took to launch me into a determined training regimen that culminated in a tear-filled but ultimately successful race in 2006, which in turn lead to an entire year of training for a painful but also successful race the following year.

Now, in 2008, I found myself working my way across Flathorn Lake for a third time. I had become an established Alaskan, an established snow biker, a person who believed, at least in theory, that I had what it took to ride past the reaches of the Susitna 100, over the Alaska Range and all the way to McGrath. I had yet to grasp the origin of the drive that brought me back to that place, again and again.

Even Bill Merchant's simple but Zen explanation — "This trail gets under your skin" — didn't begin to justify the familiarity and peace I felt in the midst of the vast and unknown surroundings of the Iditarod Trail. Or how much beauty I experienced as the orange sunlight turned the tips of the spruce trees to incandescent candles and cast long shadows over the frozen lake. The kind of beauty you never see in a brochure.

Even in February, the early Alaska sunset could still cast the sky in warm light. A deep red alpenglow reflected off far-away mountains in the Alaska Range as I crossed Dismal Swamp. Dismal Swamp was where I had my big moment during the 2006 Susitna 100 — a complete emotional meltdown.

I was trying to ride a full-suspension, "skinny tire" mountain bike through the soft snow and I had been failing miserably at it. I was sinking, falling, swimming, stumbling and swearing every few hundred feet. I felt I was the unsuspecting victim of poor gear choices and stark inexperience, and to top it all off, it was raining — something I never thought I'd see in this part of Alaska in February.

The falling rain turned the snow to almost unwalkable mush. Dismal Swamp ate me alive. Something broke. I broke. I fell off my bike a final time, knelt into the snow, and just sat there. I did not cry. I was beyond crying. Crying would have conveyed hope, and I had none. I put my head down and thought about sleep. The rain poured down. Everything I was wearing, and everything I had in my gear bags, including all of my survival gear, was completely soaked. And it was not warm. 37, maybe 38 degrees. I began to shiver. As my shivering became more pronounced, I looked up and realized that hopelessness was not an option. Being broken was not an option. Moving, no matter how slow, no matter how hard or frustrating, was my only option. So I got up. And I started walking. And continued walking. And it took me 11 more hours to cover the rest of the race course, all 30 miles of it, by slogging through a seemingly endless expanse of slush.

That moment in Dismal Swamp stands out, because it was there that I first conquered the tyranny of The Iditarod Trail. It was the most satisfying thing I had ever done.

But in 2008, 30 miles into what I believed to be my greatest challenge yet, I was coasting easy and feeling as though nothing could possibly go wrong. The Iditarod Trail had been unbelievably kind this time, and I thanked it out loud, while repeatedly chanting the word "Denali" at the massive peak glowing a brilliant pink in the distance. Seeing Mount Denali was a sign of good things to come: comfortably cool weather, sunny skies, and hardpacked trails all the way to McGrath.

What had I been so worried about? This race was going to be easy. The thought of it made me smile, as did the realization how ridiculous such thoughts were a mere 30 miles into a 350-mile race of this magnitude.

Darkness sank in as I crossed the Susitna River and began pedaling up the Yentna River, a wide, frozen highway surrounded by steep bluffs. I could see the flicker of snowmobile lights in the distance. They had packed in a wonderful trail, and I did not mind their presence in the least. The temperature began to drop and I finally started to feel comfortable in my layers. It was the same clothing I considered my base for the best conditions possible in Juneau, but I had learned it was too many layers for a day full of the best conditions possible on the Iditarod Trail — 20 degrees and sunny.

I later learned the temperature dropped to minus 10 on the river that night, and I never changed a thing about my minimal clothing. How quickly we become products of our environment.

As the scenery faded beneath the blanket of night, I retreated deeper into the landscape of my mind. I imagined I was paddling a little canoe down a great river, and at the end I would find my home. I did not know what home was. I imagined McGrath, an oasis in the desert, a warm yellow glow emanating through a howling storm. I thought about all of the amazing food I would eat in McGrath as I gnawed on a half-frozen Clif Bar until it was thawed enough to chew. I sat upright and let the cold wind stream through my bare fingers outside my handlebar mitts as I thought about the oppressive heat of the Salt Lake Valley and an old home that was so far away, and so long ago.

Beneath the monotone hues of night, the Yentna River looked like the surface of the moon. The real moon burned harvest orange behind me. I could not help but crane my neck around and look backward just to gaze at it.

I arrived at Skwentna Roadhouse, mile 90, just shy of 2 a.m. I had been pedaling for most of the past 12 hours. I had let my apprehension about the unknown sink into an acceptance of my situation, and quickly adopted it as my lifestyle. I emerged at mile 90 feeling amazing and complete. I had been alone and not seen a single other person, save for a short stop at the relatively quiet 57-mile checkpoint, since the very start of the race.

The chaos of Skwentna Roadhouse was startling and strange. The strongmen of the cyclists had slept a couple hours and were already filtering back out into the cold, ready to tackle the next section of trail. As I beamed at them and greeted them like an overly cheery receptionist, they mostly just grumbled and grunted — strong men of few words. I settled into a brightly lit dining room at a table with a red checkered tablecloth.

The lodge owner brought me a plate of spaghetti. I didn't understand how an entire plate of spaghetti — meatballs, glass plate and all — could exist this far out in the wilderness. It seemed a million miles from the bustle of the Knik Bar, light years from my home in Juneau. The lodge owner asked me if I wanted anything to drink.

"Do you have Diet Pepsi?" I croaked in my race-hoarse voice.

"You're in a bike race," she answered. "Do you really want diet?"

"I love Diet Pepsi," I answered. She had a point. I needed every calorie I could get my hands on, but right then, what I wanted most was something comfortable and familiar. Something close to home. She brought me a light blue can, glistening with droplets of water. The cold, artificially sweetened liquid inside tasted like the elixir of life.

Strongman Jay Petervary was finishing up a large bowl of soup as I sipped my soda. He asked me to take his picture in the kitchen.

"You about to take off?" I asked him.

"Yeah," he said. "I had a good three hours of sleep. Have to rest up if I'm going to race to Nome." His eyes darted around the room wildly as he spoke to me, as though he didn't even see me because he was already miles down the trail.

After the 350-mile race, there are always a handful of experienced competitors that push on toward Nome, a small town on the Bering Sea that also was the terminus of the Iditarod Trail Sled Dog Race. The human-powered race to Nome, all 1,100 miles of it, was something I couldn't even fathom. Nor was the idea that three hours of sleep was somehow a lot. Jay seemed so intense and I wondered if he could keep up his pace. But I believed he could because he was famous in these circles, so I knew he had completed races like this before.

Jay left with another cyclist just after 3 a.m., a time that had no meaning to them because in a race like this, time doesn't matter. Only distance. As the strongmen disappeared into the dark, my doubt came creeping back. If the intensity, the sleeplessness, the determination and talent that led to fame — if that's what it took to finish the race, what chance did I stand?

GHOST TRAILS

New York, New York
December 26, 2000

I had never thought of myself as a particularly strong or spontaneous person, but I liked the idea of striving for such traits.

So when I received an e-mail from my friend, Anna, asking what I thought about taking a trip to spend New Years 2001 in Syracuse, New York with her friends, I was quick to hit the reply button.

"Count me in!" I typed. "What do I need to do?"

She wrote back with a link to an online auction site where I could find deeply discounted airline tickets. She wrote that it was the cheapest way go, but we would have to commit without knowing the exact times we would fly, and we would probably not end up on the same planes. I was 21 years old and had never flown alone before. I had only been to the East Coast once on a family vacation. But with that information, I surfed over to Anna's recommended Web site and put in a bid of $200 for an end-of-year flight from Salt Lake City to New York. The site came back and asked me where in New York I wanted to fly. When I checked Syracuse, the site came back and told me there were no flights available. I wondered how close Syracuse was to the big city. I decided New York was one of those East Coast states and they were all small. How far away could it be? I could take a bus. New York City it was.

The Web site accepted my bid and came back with a flight that left early in the afternoon on Christmas Day and returned a week later. I e-mailed Anna the good news. She didn't reply until the next day.

"Oh," the letter began. "Turns out I can't go until next week. Sorry."

I was devastated. "Next week?" I wrote back. "I can't go next week." Christmas Day was just two days away. I had just spent $200, nearly an entire week's pay at my part-time job, on a nonrefundable plane ticket. I also had already basically thrown away another week's pay informing my employer that I "urgently" had to fly to New York, securing a week of unpaid leave. No, I was going on a New Years vacation. I set to work calling Anna's friends, who were acquaintances of mine but who I didn't really know that well, to work out the awkward details of my spontaneous holiday.

"New York City is a five-hour drive from Syracuse," Anna's and my mutual friend, Jen, told me over the phone. "And my parents live an hour north of there. You should definitely still come out. But I'm sorry, I can't come pick you up at the airport on Christmas."

I began to study the ugly realities of travel, of train tickets that cost more than my flight, of taxis and subways and Greyhound buses, none of which were able to get me anywhere near Syracuse on Christmas Day, and none of which I could even really afford. I was just about to scrap the entire idiotic idea when Jen called me at 5 a.m. Christmas Eve, 30 hours before my flight was scheduled to leave.

"Is it kind of early there? Sorry. But hey, my friend Geoff, he's up here for the holidays too. He'll come pick you up at the airport."

I knew Geoff, vaguely, as a friend of Jen and Anna's who usually traveled all over the country in a small truck, going to concerts and making his living selling hemp jewelry to hippies and prep school kids. He had spent the summer and most of the fall in Salt Lake, crashing at Jen's house.

I went on a camping trip to the San Rafael Swell in November with about a dozen people, and Geoff had been part of the crowd. We climbed a sandstone pinnacle in the desert and stood at the top looking across the snow-dusted landscape, and I remember he spent most of the that time laughing and joking with a 5-year-old boy. I thought I had been bowling with him once, too, but I couldn't quite remember.

I thanked Jen for the offer and started packing, but I still felt dubious at best. Was this near stranger, a friend of a friend of a friend, really going to drive six hours to pick me up in New York City late in the evening on Christmas Day? I didn't really believe it, but I didn't have much left to lose.

The plane touched down at LaGuardia International Airport at 11:47 p.m. Dec. 25. The city's skyline was shrouded in haze. I pressed my forehead against the window to catch my first glimpse of Manhattan, but couldn't make out any tall buildings in a blur of muted light. The pilot announced we would have to wait on the tarmac for a gate to open. The scattered passengers in the nearly empty plane sat back and waited.

Twenty minutes passed. Then 45. I could feel beads of sweat forming on my forehead as I gazed at the terminal that was only a few hundred feet from where we sat, completely trapped. Was Geoff inside that building, waiting? Would he continue to wait? If I were him, I probably would be halfway back to Syracuse right now, swearing up a storm at Jen for talking me into this mess. I'd probably have to find that Greyhound bus after all. Or maybe I would hitchhike. Or maybe just wait in the airport until it was time to catch my return flight. I looked down at my hands, which were starting to shake a little. I was alone in New York City. Frightened.

At 1:07 a.m., the plane lurched forward, startling me out of my concentrated breathing and deep worry. I was one of the last people to walk off the plane into an empty terminal. As my fellow passengers fanned out, I came to the stomach-sinking realization that there was no one left but me.

I slumped against a wall and looked back at the exit ramp when I noticed a man walking toward me. Geoff — at least I was pretty sure it was Geoff — emerged from the exit ramp where I had just come from. I must have walked right by him. I finally recognized his auburn beard and long brown hair — a memory from bowling, maybe, because he had been wearing a hat during our camping trip in November. He had a confused look on his face, but he was smiling.

"Why were you out there for so long?" he asked.

"They wouldn't let us off the plane."

"Why?"

"I don't know. We were waiting for the gate to clear or something."

Geoff pressed his lips as he looked around. "There's absolutely nobody else here."

"I know. It was like some kind of twilight zone episode, the one with the people cage. No reason to it at all."

He frowned. "I didn't know it was going to be so late."

"I know," I said. "I'm sorry. I'm really sorry. You didn't have to come pick me up. I would have taken the bus."

He smiled. "Yeah, but that would have sucked."

"You're not mad?"

He looked confused again. "No. Why would I be mad?"

"It's just ... we're like five hours from where you live."

"It's more like six," he said.

As we walked out to the car, I explained the mix-up with Anna, the diabolical Internet con that saddled me with a plane ticket I wasn't going to be able to use otherwise, but how I had never really seen New York and this seemed like the perfect opportunity. I apologized for getting Geoff mixed up in the whole mess.

"You've never seen New York?"

"Not really," I said. "I drove through here once with my family when I was 15 or so. I was so surly about being 15 and being stuck with my family for a week that I don't remember much about it."

"You should," he said. "You should see New York."

We left the airport and drove through neighborhoods and over a bridge, emerging deep in a canyon of tall buildings. Geoff pulled his car next to the curb and stopped. I still had my cheek against the window, unable to stop looking up. Bright signs climbing hundreds of feet into the air advertised Coca Cola and Broadway. Mountains of city lights stamped out any semblance of night that I knew. The street was so bright that I could read painted storefront signs that were blocks away. The lights also illuminated the emptiness of the city, with entire blocks devoid of pedestrians or cars.

"Where are we?" I asked Geoff as we stepped outside. A blast of cold air burrowed in to my meager layers — holey jeans, a T-shirt and a cotton hoodie.

"Times Square," Geoff said.

"I thought there'd be people here," I said.

"Usually there are a ton of people here. I guess not so much at 2 a.m. on Christmas."

"Really, it's December 26 now," I said as I opened the back door and pulled a snowboarding jacket and hat from my checked baggage. I dug deeper but I could not find gloves. Had a forgotten gloves?

"Man, it's cold," I said. "How cold do you think it is?"

"I don't know," Geoff said as he pulled on a thick coat and gloves. "Probably about 10 degrees."

"Holy cow," I said. "I don't think I've ever been anywhere this cold. I mean, sometimes it drops down to single digits at Brighton when we go night skiing. But we're always really bundled up when at night, plus we're snowboarding, and that keeps you pretty warm." I gazed up at the pinnacle of glowing advertisements. "I've seen that somewhere before."

"Probably in movies."

I looked up again. "Oh yeah, this place is pretty famous. Times Square. As in New Year's Eve Times Square?"

"Yeah. But trust me, you don't want to be here on New Years. It's a mad zoo."

"Yeah, better to be here now," I laughed and shivered. "At least now you can get a parking space."

A low moaning breeze swept through the concrete corridors. Not a single car had driven by in five minutes. Snow flurries fluttered around us as we walked up the empty sidewalk. Storefronts were shuttered and dark. Thick clouds of pungent steam rose up from subway grates. Traffic lights were perpetually green. The city seemed vast and empty, like the desert, and I couldn't believe how familiar it all felt.

"Who knew New York was a ghost town?" I said. "I feel like we're in one of those last-people-on-earth movies."

"In a way, we are," Geoff said. We walked by a time and temperature sign. The digital display flashed 5 degrees, 2:14 a.m.

"Is that 5 degrees Celsius?"

"No, that's 5 degrees flat."

"I didn't think it ever got this cold right next to the ocean," I said.

"You're thinking of the West Coast," Geoff said.

We rounded a street corner and walked toward an open expanse of dark space. Street lights flickering above the sidewalk illuminated trees and paths. "That's Central Park," Geoff said. "Usually you never go into Central Park after dark. But right now, I dunno, no one around; it's probably OK."

"Sweet!" I said. "Times Square! Central Park! Wait until I tell my mom about all of the places I visited. She'll be jealous."

We left the street and walked into the shadows, on a path that circled a small reservoir. The tree cover thickened but I could still see the sparkling peaks of the city's skyline. I picked up my pace to a near jog and Geoff followed close behind. My toes, wrapped only in a single set of cotton socks and skate shoes, felt heavy and numb. My thighs tingled against stiff and icy denim. I held my arms tight against my sides, my gloveless fingers clenched in the pockets of my thin coat.

There was no amount of exertion that was actually going to warm me up, but I did not want to leave this place, this beautiful city that Geoff and I had all to ourselves.

"So you grew up in New York?" I said.

"Yeah, north of Syracuse," he said. "You'll see. It's nowhere near here."

"And that's how you know Jen?"

"We went to high school together."

"I met Jen in college," I said. "And Anna. We were all in this environmentalist club, Terra Firma. A bunch of the people in the club got this house, commune style."

"I know," he said. "I was living there."

"Right," I said. "So you're living there now? I thought you mostly traveled around."

"Mostly," he said. "But I've been in Utah on and off since March. I left in the fall, but I'm going to go back after the holidays."

"So, you're done traveling?"

"No. I just want to spend some more time around Utah."

"So what do you do when you're traveling?"

"I go to concerts, like Dave Matthews and Rusted Root concerts. Make jewelry. Drive and see different places. I go running and hiking. Sometimes backpacking. I read a lot."

"All by yourself?"

"I go on trips with friends," he said, "but, yeah, a lot of the time I'm by myself."

"Man, I had a hard enough time getting on that plane by myself," I said. "When my parents found out I was flying alone and not with Anna, I thought they were going to handcuff me and drag me kicking and screaming away from the airport."

"How old are you?"

"21," I said. "Full-fledged college graduate, too"

"Do you have a job?"

"I'm a catalog and brochure designer for this art and frame company," I said. "But I'm trying to get into newspapers. I think I may have a shot at this job at a weekly paper in Murray. Yeah, Murray's a town in suburban Salt Lake."

"That's cool. Do you like your job now?"

"Yeah," I said. "Mostly, I just want to find something full time. I mean, I haven't stopped working since the week I turned 16. Jobs all the time. Sometimes I have two."

"I haven't worked a full-time job since I was about 17," Geoff said and smiled. "Nearly eight years."

"And you can get by selling jewelry?"

"I make pretty good money. Enough for food and gas, everything that matters."

We returned to the beginning of our reservoir loop and re-entered the pavement, cast in pale yellow beneath the street lights. The tingling in my legs had subsided, and I noticed as I relaxed my fists that my whole body seemed to be acclimating to the cold. I couldn't help but laugh quietly about the whole situation. There I was, suburban Utah girl, first big trip away from home, walking around big bad New York City with a virtual stranger, in the middle of the night, in the dead of winter, and feeling more and more comfortable with it by the minute.

"Do you ever think about traveling?" Geoff asked me.

"You mean, like quit my job, buy a Euro-train pass, backpack across Asia and canoe down the Amazon?"

"Something like that," Geoff said.

"I don't know," I said. "I've definitely thought about it. I've come pretty close a few times. I even got a passport. But I just never felt like one of those people who needed to travel across the world just to find myself. Don't get me wrong, I love vacations. But I like them in small doses, little tastes of new places to help break up the routine at home."

"If you had a million dollars, would you still sit around Salt Lake and work?"

I considered it for a second, but said, "yeah, I'd still work. Less, but, I like Salt Lake. Even though I grew up there, it just feels like the perfect place for me. And I like working. It keeps me grounded. Gives me more purpose than just sitting around and going snowboarding once in a while."

"And it's not about money?"

"No," I said. "I mean, I'm trying to be a journalist. You don't really make money doing that. But I do like food and shelter."

"Cause, you know, money really doesn't matter," Geoff said. "You don't need a whole lot for food and shelter. You can eat grilled cheese and sleep in a tent."

"I don't like grilled cheese."

"Well, I already have more money than I need," Geoff said. "I probably have

$10,000. You can have it if you need it. It just accumulates with me. I'll give it to you."

"I don't need your money," I laughed. "It's bad enough you had to come pick me up in this remote outpost."

"Well, you should really get out and see the world sometime."

"Yeah," I said. "But, well ..." I pointed up at the towering buildings. "I'm already on my way. I'm seeing New York."

"You've seen the city," he said. "No one from upstate thinks of this as New York. I'll show you New York."

A small sedan with a roaring muffler rumbled by us just as a woman in the passenger's seat rolled the window down and screamed "Merry Christmas!"

"And Happy New Year!" I yelled back with all the enthusiasm I genuinely felt, because I knew it was going to be an exciting week.

Skwentna River, Alaska
February 25, 2008

Exactly one and a half hours after eating, brushing my teeth, stripping off all of my lightly frosted layers and hanging them around the room to dry before collapsing into bed, I woke up ... without prompting.

My digital camera, with an alarm set for 8 a.m., sat silently on the dresser. The time was just before 6 a.m. It was Monday.

I blinked against a bright glare and realized I had forgotten to turn off the overhead light. I felt much worse than I had before I went to sleep. My heart was beating too quickly. The veins in my legs were throbbing, and my muscles felt disconcertingly like mush. I laid down and wondered if I should go back to sleep, but my body was too amped up — and exhausted. Plus, 6 a.m. seemed like a good time to hit the trail again. I got out of bed and went to work reapplying my layers. Some of them were still a bit damp.

I stumbled into the bathroom and looked in the mirror. I still looked strangely ... normal. Bloodshot eyes and a pasty face, but, otherwise ... normal. I did not know what I had expected myself to look like after my first day of the Iditarod race. I think I had pictured blackened cheeks or some kind of shell-shocked facial expression. In all of the months leading up to the event, I could never quite visualize my body in the actual race beyond the horrifying if exaggerated images in movies about Arctic expeditions. I think this may have been a coping mechanism that helped me separate myself from the overwhelming reality of the future ... by making it theatrical.

The morning was still as black as night when I stumbled down the stairs. The same woman who made me spaghetti at 3 a.m. was still manning the kitchen. "Did you get enough sleep?" she said, eyeing me suspiciously. I nodded wearily. "All you racers don't sleep enough," she said, shaking her head. "Except that one man, Peter. He's been here since, oh, I don't know, 11 or so?"

"Wait, Pete's still here?" I said. "Pete Basinger?"

Pete Basinger was a perennial favorite in the Iditarod Trail Invitational. He had entered the race every year since the early 2000s, back when I was still suffering through short, simple day hikes and sleeping my way through a post-college haze. Pete also won the race on a regular basis, and in 2007 set the course record after an inspiring all-night push that had me glued to sporadic Internet updates. Those simple text postings sparked a personal dream about the Iditarod race, which quickly flared into an obsession. When my friends and family asked me what streak of insanity could have possibly coaxed me to enter the race, it was easy to blame Pete and the strongman way in which he made pain and suffering look so fun and easy. Naturally, I never thought I'd meet him during the race.

"Yeah," she said. "He's waiting for a bike pedal to be flown in. Last night he broke one of his pedals, and he was riding it on the spindle, and then I think the other one broke, and so he had to walk the last five or 10 miles into here."

"And he still made it by 11," I said, shaking my head with amazement. "And a full night of sleep. I bet he's pissed, isn't he?"

"He didn't seem too happy," she said. "All those other guys, those guys are long gone. He'll never catch them."

I just smiled. "I bet he will." Silently, I wished I could be at home on the Internet to watch him try.

The woman offered me breakfast. I thanked her but refused. My stomach just lurched and spun and threatened to reject anything I sent down. I blamed it on nerves. I could eat in a few hours, I decided. Another back-of-pack cyclist, Ted Calahane, was also packing up to leave as I walked out of the wood-heated building. The cold air outside slammed into me like a solid wall of ice. I gasped for breath and rushed to my bike, which was already whitewashed in hoarfrost. The air was windless, the morning as still as death.

I couldn't believe I had somehow survived a night in these temperatures just hours before. I was still wearing all the same clothing, but I felt like I would freeze solid if I slowed my movement for even a second. I packed quickly and pulled on my mittens. Adding more layers seemed like too much of an ordeal unless I went back inside the cabin, and I did not want to admit to the woman that I was too cold to even start the day. She didn't seem to approve of my quick nap and just might not release me again. I decided the situation would improve if I just started riding. I took a quick glance at the thermometer. The red line hovered around

12 or 13 below.

Ted and I rode along the short road together before it veered onto a trail across a flat, open swamp. I could see purple streaks of dawn hugging the hills directly ahead — the Shell Hills. I had hoped to stick with Ted for most of the morning, but my legs were still stiff and weak, and I had to push too hard just to stay behind him. I let him gain a gap on me, until all I could see was the pale white glow of his headlamp hundreds of yards distant, and then I couldn't even see that.

Warmth began to return as morning broke and the real climbing began. I followed fresh snowmobile tracks as they veered sharply up the hills. I could hear streams gurgling beneath the snow under my feet, even at sub-zero temperatures. Moose tracks punctured the trail. I could tell a lot of them had been planted since even the last cyclists came through.

I looked around nervously in the soft light. Too many Alaskans have told me moose would rather stomp me than let me walk by them, and I regarded the presence of moose with the same apprehension that I felt toward bears in the summer. But I didn't see any hulking brown bodies moving beside me ... only the spindly spruce and alder, and a snowy expanse bathed in pink light.

I pushed my bike over the last big pitch and started dropping toward a frozen lake a few hundred feet below. Ill-advised, daring downhill runs would become a theme for this section of trail, even though my technical skills failed to keep up with my confidence surges. I was always so happy any time I could ride my bike, especially if I had been walking it for a while, that I didn't even care if I was careening down a narrow trail, fishtailing wildly and only one hard brake away from a big-air endo. I was going to ride any time it was possible to keep the wheels on top of the snow. So ride I did, banking on blind luck as I recklessly attacked the tight turns and tear-inducing descents out of the Shell Hills.

After I dropped onto Shell Lake, I caught up with Ted. He was fumbling around with his bags and shivering violently.

"I need to put on more clothing," he told me. "This wind is killing me." I turned my face to meet the cross wind that we had been bucking. On the only bare skin I had exposed, the bridge of my nose, the wind did indeed feel like the blunt side of a fist.

"Have you been down here for a while?"

"About 20 minutes," he said. "I've been having a hard time with my stuff. But I had to get out of the wind."

I thought to point out that it was strange he stopped in the middle of the lake to put on more clothing rather than just ride to the other end, where there was supposedly a lodge, and even if there wasn't, there was at least the shelter of trees to help block the wind. He seemed to be struggling mightily, and I wondered if this was one of those critical trail moments I had pictured before the race, a scenario in which I might meet an incoherent, unreasonable fellow racer and would have to decide whether to continue on my way or mount a rescue effort. I pitied any racer who needed me as a rescuer, but at the same time, felt even more uncertain about assuming as much about Ted — a man, older and likely much more experienced than me — who was still conscious.

"Are you sure you're OK?" I asked. Ted nodded.

"Well, I can't stand around in this wind much longer," I said. "I'll meet you at Shell Lake Lodge? I'm headed there for breakfast."

"I don't think I'm going to stop there," Ted said. "I'd really like to get to Puntilla by nightfall."

"You think you can get there by dark?" I asked, surprised. It was only 9 a.m. Puntilla was about 50 miles away. I had hoped to achieve that checkpoint by dinner time myself, but you can never assume consistent movement along the Iditarod Trail. The Iditarod Trail alone decides how fast you move and when you will reach checkpoints. I personally would never voice my goals out loud where the vengeful Iditarod Trail Powers That Be could hear me. Better to keep my hopes to myself, and if I achieved them, I could chalk it up to perfect luck.

"Of course," he said, beginning to sound exasperated with me. I could tell he was becoming suspicious of my concern, and he didn't appreciate it.

"Great," I said. The chill was starting the creep into my layers, so I waved a goodbye with my mittens and continued on.

I was still not hungry at the Shell Lake Lodge, which didn't seem possible. I had forced myself to consume exactly half a Clif Bar sometime around 6 a.m., and one of my 12 precious peanut butter cups since then. But I had been awake for nearly four hours, and traveling for more than three, and I really should have had more of an appetite than those 300 calories could fulfill.

The lodge was warm but not toasty. I felt uncomfortably cold sitting around it my wet clothes. I stripped my outermost layers and laid them next to the wood stove as a soft-spoken woman brought me coffee even though I had not yet asked for it. I took a long, savoring sip as she told me about the racers who had already been through that morning and the weather they expected to see during the day. Her words faded into the background as I slipped into comfort food oblivion. Hot, caffeinated and calorie free, the coffee was the most delicious thing I had consumed since my Diet Pepsi the night before.

I ordered the only breakfast they offered — bacon and eggs, something I would never in a million years eat at home — and sat next to one of several Euro cyclists who all spoke very little English and whose names I could never remember.

I drifted in an out of daydreams for the seeming hours it took the woman to make our breakfast, which she brought to us at the same time even though the Euro cyclist could have arrived at the lodge hours before me for all I knew. We sat together at the same table in the otherwise empty dining room, wordlessly spooning greasy morsels of fuel into our mouths and smiling occasionally because we could not communicate otherwise.

My breakfast tasted like ash and bile. I did not think it was the cook's fault. I was simply in one of my typical endurance cycling food funks. I had experienced a similar inability to take in food during long rides before, and sometimes wasn't able to start eating again until I was done riding. But I didn't worry too much about it at the time because I knew I still had days in which I could recover my appetite. With my endurance racing time now measured not in minutes or hours, but days, my body didn't really have a choice.

I was picking slowly at the eggs and trying to think about something besides the urge to vomit when Ted sauntered into the building, looking, for lack of a better cliche, like death warmed over. I had passed him less than one mile from the lodge. More than an hour had gone by since he told me he planned to bypass the building, so my concern jumped to the forefront of my thoughts again. I pushed away my half-eaten breakfast, picked up my coffee, and walked toward him.

"You OK?" I asked.

"I took a wrong turn," he said. "I went about three miles up the lake before the trail just kind of ended, and I saw a guy on a snowmachine who pointed me back here."

He looked really unhappy. His face was scrunched up like a picked-on child who was struggling not to cry.

"That sucks. But you're OK, right?" I asked. He nodded miserably and started taking off his boots. I thought he might quit right there at the Shell Lake Lodge, and I wasn't about to try to stop him. In those early days of the race, when I was still feeling relatively strong and had no idea how deep one really needs to dig into the pain cave just to survive the Iditarod Trail, I might have even encouraged it.

But at that moment, I was feeling sick and sleepy and knew that as long as he was in a building, Ted was in better hands than mine. I began to gather up my clothing and headed back out the door into the bright morning. I had burned up well over an hour procuring that horrible breakfast, but I must have pushed some of it down because my energy level was hitting new highs. Instead of exploiting it, I sat back and rode easy, turning my face to the perfect blue sky and savoring each breath of frigid air. Ted passed me on the trail less than a mile later and churned on ahead. He was still pushing his planned schedule.

Alone again, I quietly spun over the smooth snow. All around me, the jagged peaks of the Alaska Range loomed much closer than they had the night before. The trail into the mountains seemed like such a long approach — already a lifetime had passed since I had lined up in Knik the day before. And yet I was surprised how quickly I had reached the distant horizon.

In any other lifetime, the Alaska backcountry would have been an unobtainable fortress, surrounded by the wall of my own inexperience. That I could just sit on a bicycle and power myself into the heart of such a remote, empty wilderness made me feel proud — and fearful. If I could pedal myself this far into the backcountry, what was to stop me from pedaling beyond the point of no return?

I had the Finger Lake Lodge, mile 130, in sight when I heard footprints approaching behind me. I looked over my shoulder and saw Pete Basinger himself, pushing his bike through the soft spur trail that led to the lodge. His clothing looked clean and pressed, like it had just come out of a dryer, instead of being worn over 130 slow and snowy miles. His curly brown hair clung to his scalp, wet and glistening in the "heat" of mid-day. Even for a big guy, his lightly loaded bike looked like a featherweight compared to mine, and I could see it had two pedals. Knowing he likely had to wait until at least 9 a.m. for a mail plane to land before he could even fix his bike, I was amazed that he had caught me already.

"Hi," I said, with a nervous smile. I couldn't let Pete know I worshiped him in the way other sports fans worship Lance Armstrong or Michael Jordan. It seemed completely ridiculous to harbor such pretentions in a sport this small — ultra-endurance snow biking — that I was in the presence of the greatest athlete in the world, but I couldn't help but stammer like a star-struck schoolgirl. "So you were able to fix your bike?"

"Yeah," he said. "It's fixed." He moved quickly past me. Of course he didn't have time to chat with me, a lowly, back-of-pack fan. He had a peloton to catch.

Inside the lodge, I grabbed some lunch with two other racers: Brij Potnis, one of the strongmen who was purposefully taking long breaks and essentially "touring" the Iditarod Trail, and Ted, who was sitting at the table red-eyed and shaking and not even looking at the plate of food in front of him. Pete turned down the free lunch and began rifling through his drop bag, a 10-pound sack of goodies that every racer is allowed to ship to themselves at mile 130 and mile 210. I stole glances to see what pros like Pete used in this race. Inside Pete's bag, I saw mostly candy bars and chocolate. There were even Twizzlers and some type of color-coated cartoon candy that I've never seen anyone older than 9 purchase.

So that was the food of champions, I thought, and I smiled knowingly. My Power Bars and mixed nuts suddenly seemed idiotic. I wasn't eating them; I was only carrying them like dead weight into the frozen wilderness. Meanwhile, I hoarded my limited peanut butter cups like an unreasonable miser and consumed my body's fat stores just to continue the forward motion.

Pete started switching memory cards on his mp3 player. I asked him what music he was listening to. "I don't know," he said. "Mostly crap."

And with that, he stood up, gathered his pile of candy and crappy music, and rushed out the door. I wondered if I would ever have a chance to tell him how cool it was for me to see him for that short time out on the trail, out in the middle of nowhere in the heart of his element. It seemed childish and ridiculous, but running into Pete was a highlight of my trip.

Back out on the trail after 5 p.m., I joined Brij and the Euro cyclist I had eaten breakfast with as we began the long walk into the Alaska Range. Ted opted to stay behind at Finger Lake Lodge. "I need a nap," Ted had told us. "I can't keep my eyes open."

Brij, the unassuming strongman, quickly put the gap on the Euro cyclist and me. We resumed our line of two and walked together silently up the steep, soft pitch as darkness fell.

After about a half hour of silence in the twilight, the Euro cyclist surprised me by speaking his first words of English to me — "So, The Push!"

I nodded — The Push. We had been warned that Finger Lake to Puntilla gained the most elevation of any section of the trail. It was time to walk, so walk we did. The Euro cyclist walked faster than I did, so eventually I was alone again.

The rest of the night passed by in a blur. I was so tired I felt like laying down in the snow to sleep, but so amped up that my heart was pumping at a rate I would have considered 80 or 85 percent of my maximum — running levels — even though I was walking slowly up relatively mild hills. The snail pace was frustrating, so I tried riding every few hundred yards. I found pedaling to be possible often enough, but much more physically difficult than it was usually worth. The route climbed and dropped on a series of steep rollercoaster hills as it made its way toward a place called Happy Valley. I hit a few descents at fever pace, with my tiny yellow headlamp bobbing up and down into the inky night as spruce and alder branches whisked inches from my head.

I bottomed out in the Happy River gorge and discovered I could not climb back out. The trail shot up a bluff on a nearly vertical pitch. I tried pushing my bike up the middle of the trail, but I slid and tumbled back down a number of times.

I tried stepping into the untracked snow off to the side of the trail, only to sink to my thighs in the powder, unable to take another step. Finally, I turned my 70-pound bike on its side, kicked my own stairway into the hillside, and dragged my bike up the wall, step by excruciating step, as the pedals dug in to the snow and prevented too much backsliding. It was a 20-foot section of trail that took me a half hour to conquer. And I still had a lot of elevation to climb before I reached Puntilla Lake. I let out a long sigh. I was officially crawling.

My frozen breath swirled in thick clouds around my face and turned my balaclava into an icy helmet. After what seemed like days of walking toward a spotlight in an endlessly dark room, I reached the edge of Puntilla Lake. My eyes burned as I walked around the last clump of trees and dropped onto the open lake, where the wind hit my face like fire. I pulled out my thermometer. It was hovering somewhere between 15 and 20 below. Even before windchill, that was officially the coldest temperature I had ever experienced. I was somewhat heartened by the thought that it really didn't feel so bad.

I pulled into Puntilla Lake lodge just as the strongmen of the race were preparing to leave again after another short night's sleep. Pete had already left without sleep. The last of the strongmen stopped to wish me well before he disappeared into the 4 a.m. darkness.

"I feel pretty much awful," I told him.

He just smiled. "You made it here," he said. "You're as good as already there."

I decided I believed him, because at that point, I had no choice.

GHOST TRAILS

Cataract Canyon, Utah
April 14, 2001

My hands were already calloused, my fear softened when our small expedition of friends reached the headwaters of Utah's biggest rapids.

I pulled hard on the oars and pointed Geoff's raft toward a narrow strip of land where the mint candy-colored waters of the Green River met the hot cocoa patina of the muddy Colorado. The boat plowed into a sandbar as Geoff jumped over the front and ran a rope up to a stand of tamarisk. Bryan stood in the opaque water and started the lunch chores, ferrying a cooler, a table and a couple dry bags out of Geoff's raft. I rubbed the dry skin on my upper arms, which felt feverishly warm beneath the April sun.

"Rowing is hard," I announced as Chris and his crew pulled their raft up on shore next to us.

"Rowing the flatwater is easy," Chris said. "Wait until we start hitting the rapids."

"Oh, I'm not going to row any of those," I said. "Even if Geoff were willing to let me handle his boat, which he won't, but I wouldn't. I'm pretty sure I'd just dump us all in the drink."

"You should get Geoff to let you row some of the first rapids," Chris said. "This river pools and drops, so there's usually a chance to pull over and scout lines. The rapids pretty much get bigger and wilder as you go, but some of the numbered rapids are pretty easy. You just point the boat into the current and go. You could do it blindfolded."

"That's good, because that's about my skill level," I said. "But I think I'll pass. I'm happy to let Geoff have the fun. How many of those numbered rapids are there?"

"I don't know ... about 20," Chris said. "Rapids one through seven or so are mostly pretty straightforward, wave trains and stuff. Then you start going through some bigger holes."

"The Big Drops?" I asked.

"After the numbered ones, you get to the Big Drops," Chris said and grinned sheepishly. "Those are the crazy waterfalls that lose an insane amount of river elevation all at once. Wait till you see them. They earn their names."

The Big Drops were heralded almost exclusively in every piece of literature I had skimmed about Cataract Canyon. Terrified as I was about Geoff's proposed spring rafting trip and the prospect of willfully riding a rubber boat over the cold, churning water, I agreed to go anyway. I tempered my fear by looking at every Utah rafting book I could find at the library. I consulted their tips. I gleaned their recommendations. I took their general opinions as gospel, and, in general, most said the Colorado River was probably not going to crush me.

The specific reviews were a bit more ominous. The Big Drops, three of them, were the inspiration of many river legends and the proprietors of a handful of deaths. "Experts only," one book warned. "Guide recommended," said another. Geoff assured me that all of the deaths happened during flood years and really big water; this was early spring and the river was still running well below peak velocity.

"Most of the rapids are just little bumps this time of year," Geoff had said. "You'll see huge rocks out of the water that are normally covered by holes. Trust me, you'll love rafting. It's just being in the desert, deep in the canyon, camping and cooking with your friends. It's the coolest feeling."

He smiled with a sincerity I couldn't resist. Geoff had recently fallen in love with rafting himself, not long after he returned to Utah from New York. He took one weekend trip with Chris and immediately started shopping around for boats. Just a month before, he had driven all the way to Mesquite, Nevada, and paid $3,500 cash for what was essentially a 14-foot red rubber toy. He had been taking near-weekly trips both with Chris and alone ever since. Geoff was a novice oarsman at best, but Chris insisted he was a natural.

"He'll be rowing better than me by the end of the summer," Chris had assured me. "Trust me, he's really good."

So peer pressure was the reason I found myself boarding Geoff's raft at a put-in point 50 miles upriver from the confluence of the Green and Colorado rivers. The put-in was the last time the road met the river before the legendary rapids. That reality meant that once we hit the rapids, we were many long days away from help. It also meant we had several days of flatwater to contend with before we even hit our first rapids, so I had plenty more time to sit on the boat and stew about my fears.

Anxiety whipped up a churning in my stomach that made it difficult to eat much or sleep at all during the lazy days and nights. But as we floated farther into the wilderness, I found myself resting a little deeper, opening more of my thoughts to the towering scenery and even laughing with my friends as they joked about whitewater swimming. Geoff showed me how to push and pull the oars, how to shimmy the boat sideways or spin off an eddy. I took my turns at the helm, and when the heat and the effort started to sink below the skin, I would plunge into the milk chocolate-colored river and swim alongside the raft, breathing deeply as the gritty water caressed my skin and tiny catfish nibbled on my feet.

Early in the evening, we'd pull up on a sandbar and unload a mountain of dry bags from the boats. We cooked elaborate meals and ate and drank late into the night as driftwood-fueled fires illuminated the canyon walls. As the lazy days and nights wore on, I watched as Geoff, my brand new friend and even newer full-time resident of Utah, opened up fully in the midst of his natural environment. After a few nights of laying in the sand, divulging our life stories to each other and the stars, we were old friends. And after a few days of rowing a raft over the calm surface of the Colorado, we were old river hands.

Still in the back of my mind, the Big Drops loomed. As fearsome as their names and reputations were, I couldn't quite figure out why those particular rapids had such a strong grip on my thoughts. Despite the harrowing tales, the books I had read made whitewater rafting seem safe and normal enough. I knew I could trust my friends and was beginning to believe I could trust Geoff most of all. But early in the morning, as Geoff went out for his daily run and the rest of the group slept in the sand, I would lie awake, listening to the quiet trickle of the river current as I battled an undefinable dread. As much as I didn't want our idyllic calm-water vacation to end, the unfocused dread ignited a fight response that longed to charge into the heart of the Big Drops so I could finally see why they taunted me.

But as I stood at the end of the Green River and the beginning of the Colorado's famed descent into madness, the dread began to take on its own shape. The canyon walls loomed over our heads, imprisoning us in their unbroken shadows. I was still sitting on the side of the boat when Geoff returned from the anchor trees. He directed me to help him lift the last dry box out of the frame.

"Those rapids," I said. "The ones before the Big Drops. Do any of them have names?"

"Probably," Geoff said. "But most people just know them by their numbers. That's how they're marked on the map." We plopped the aluminum box down in the sand. Geoff opened it and began clanging through the dishes inside.

"So why wouldn't anyone name them?"

"I don't know," Geoff said. "Maybe because they come so fast that the Powell expedition didn't have time."

We threw together a quick lunch. Our group — Geoff, myself and Bryan on one boat; Chris, Jen, Amy and Tim on the other — gathered around the table to laugh and joke and stoke our enthusiasm for the upcoming adventure. This, after all, was the reason we had just spent three days on the river. The bonfires and the big dinners and the heart-to-hearts with Geoff were just killing time.

I ate my sandwich in silence, then slithered into my wetsuit before anyone else had even finished eating. They passed around a box of Chips Ahoy cookies.

"Better enjoy 'em," Bryan said in a mock sinister tone. "They may be your last."

We packed up and I took my place next to Bryan on the cooler at the front of Geoff's boat. Geoff, who announced it was too hot outside to row and wear a wet suit, pulled on a thin winter jacket over his T-shirt and took the helm.

It seemed like mere seconds had passed before I first heard hints of a dull roar, echoing up the canyon like a flash flood in reverse. "Here it comes," Bryan said. We rounded a bend in the river to face the roiling waves of Rapid Number One. I held my breath as the nose of the boat plunged into the first small hole.

The raft bounced wildly and Bryan let out a happy yelp. I glanced nervously over my shoulder to look at Geoff. His face was locked in red concentration; his arms rotated the oars furiously as the boat spun toward the rippling channel. We bucked and thrashed over the corduroy water until the river spat us into a swirling pool.

"Eddy!" Geoff yelled. Chris's boat, just ahead of us, was floating off to the right and seemed to have steered completely clear of it. Geoff, however, had veered right into its gut. He cranked the boat around until it spun free.

"Hit that eddy," Geoff said to Chris as we caught up to the other boat.

"Yeah, just keep following my line," Chris said. "A couple of these have some rocks at low water."

We hung on near Chris's boat through rapids two and three. My heart, which had been beating at stress level for nearly a half hour, finally began to settle into a fatigued calm. Whitewater rafting really was something like a bouncy ride, I thought. This boat was pretty good at floating and Geoff wasn't terrible at keeping it off the rocks. Bryan couldn't stop laughing and peppering me with sarcastic comments about the splashy Colorado and about how everyone thought it was so hardcore.

Chris and Geoff pulled off the river briefly before Rapid Number Four to discuss scouting, but decided it would be fine to row down river without stopping for a few more rapids. The continuous roar had finally started to fade into the oblivion of white noise. My fear was settling low. I started looking up, at the canyon and the redrock and everything beautiful that rose out of the bowels of the river. I fixed my eyes on the rim.

"It won't be long, and I'll be up there again," I thought.

GHOST TRAILS

The wave train of Rapid Number Five rolled deep and wide and Geoff sailed right down the center. I watched as Chris blasted through a wall of water, sending up an explosion of white spray. Chris veered sharply to the right and Geoff turned his raft in the same direction. With the nose pointed perpendicular to the flow, I had to veer my neck sharply to the left to see the monster crest that Chris had just plunged through. From that perspective, it looked as high as the canyon walls, blocking out the sun.

"Wow," Bryan said as he gazed up with me. "This one is going to get us wet."

I uttered an almost sincere little laugh as the side of the boat started to climb up the water wall, lifting higher and higher into the bright blue sky until everything went dark.

It was the contrast that hit me first. The Colorado River I had known, the echoing roar and glaring sun and roiling whitewater, plunged into a world of silence and black, immediate and seemingly eternal. That I could see or hear absolutely nothing startled me more than the fact I could not breathe, more than the fact my limbs were being tossed around by forces I could not fight, more than the rush of deep cold that penetrated every pore. I felt my chest heave as though an unseen force field was yanking me upward. I opened my eyes in the gritty water just in time to see streaks of blue light before my shoulder slammed into something sharp and hard.

My body swirled around and pulled again toward the blue light, when suddenly something like a rope caught my neck. My legs shot ahead as I twisted and thrashed, kicking wildly at the surface of the water. With a desperate surge of energy, I tucked my knees to my chest and spun around until the rope released its grip. My torso surged higher and my head popped out of the water like a pool toy, bobbing helpless against repeated submersion by the waves of Rapid Number Five.

Facing upstream, I could see the overturned boat drifting farther away from me. Bryan was crouched on top of it like a frog on a red lily pad, but without oars he was helpless to direct the boat anywhere. The current was carrying me quickly away. I pulled hard with my arms to spin my body so it was facing downstream, where I was certain I was about to meet the rock that would end my life. As I flailed my arms and legs around in circles, I spotted a head bobbing beside me.

"Geoff!" I gasped. "Geoff!"

"Don't panic!" he yelled. "Don't panic! Chris is coming!"

I jerked my head around, but all I could see were the towering canyon walls and the narrow sky, which looked almost white in the glare of the midday sun. From behind, I felt a new force grab the top of my life jacket and yank my ragdoll body out of the water. I kicked weakly as my skin rubbed against the hot friction of rubber and scrapped over cold metal. Tim set me down in Chris's boat, gasping and sputtering with my mouth against the floor. As I struggled to sit up, I saw Chris lassoing a bag of rope toward Bryan, who was still perched on top of Geoff's upside-down raft. Geoff grabbed a strand of webbing and launched himself out of the water. He climbed over the tube and settled on the floor beside me. When I looked up at him, he was smiling.

"Damn," he said. "Hit that one sideways. Are you all right?"

I nodded, wide-eyed and quiet.

"Hey," Amy said from her perch on a cooler above us. "You're bleeding."

"Me?" I said weakly.

"Yeah," she said, and held her hand up to her neck. I put my hand against mine. A warm trickle of liquid flowed between my fingers. I held them to my face. They were coated in translucent red, blood mixed with water.

"How did you cut your neck?" Geoff asked as he inspected the damage.

"Rope," I said. "I think I got caught in a rope."

"What rope?" Geoff frowned. "They were all tied down."

"It was some kind of rope," I said. "Right under the boat. I came up right under the boat."

"Wow, that sucks," Amy said. "But it doesn't look too bad. It's not very deep."

I glared at her. Being cut by a rope was not too bad. Being caught underwater by a rope was an experience I didn't think anyone should write off so nonchalantly. That was easily the scariest thing that had ever happened to me, and Amy was already laughing about it.

"Too bad you guys couldn't see yourselves go over," she said. "We all heard the sound and we looked over just in time to see the whole bottom of your boat, like this huge red whale jumping out of the water. It was like ... really red."

Geoff laughed. I didn't even smile. An involuntary shivering was starting to take over my facial expressions.

"You cold?" Geoff asked me as Chris rowed up to a sandbar, towing Bryan and the overturned boat behind him.

"Yeah," I said. "A little."

"Me too," Geoff said. "I don't understand how you did so much swimming in that river. That water is seriously cold."

"I didn't mean to take a swim right there," I said. "That was your brilliant move."

Geoff just wasn't grasping all of the guilt and blame I felt he owed me. He was still smiling and laughing as we crawled out of the boat and stepped with numb feet onto the hot, dry sand. Geoff, Bryan and Chris lined up against Geoff's raft and pulled together on the webbing until the boat flipped back over. They started untying the bags and boxes, dragging each one onto the sand. Chris opened Geoff's dry box.

"Water in here," he said. He pulled out a dripping T-shirt streaked in beige. "Looks like some bleach got out, too."

Geoff opened up a few dry bags. "Wet, wet, wet," he rattled off the status of all of our survival gear and current worldly belongings. "Wow, pretty much all of our stuff is wet. Gonna be fun camping out tonight."

I held my hand up to my neck and ran my fingers through the sticky blood, which was already drying against my clammy skin. My pulse was racing, responding to the immediate past and indefinite future. I was uncertain if the rush I was feeling was shock or fear or exhilaration. My new joy in the thought of just being alive was tempered by a new certainty about impending death. We had at least 15 more of these rapids to go through, and then the Big Drops, and I didn't think I could survive another swim.

Geoff said something about dry clothes and Chris said something about a fire, but all I could hear was the unrelenting roar of Rapid Number Five. It just rolled on effortlessly, merging with the quieter roars of the near future, rapids Six and Seven, and beyond that was the unknown of the river, and the deep canyon, and the Big Drops so far away that they seemed like nothing. Nothing at all.

Rainy Pass, Alaska
February 26, 2008

The Puntilla Lake Lodge was little more than a roof and a stove pipe sticking out of a small mountain of drifted snow.

Its elevation was about 2,000 feet, an unlikely altitude for human inhabitants in that part of the world. Weather that would be considered extreme anywhere else — 20 below temperatures, 40 mph wind gusts, white-out blizzards — was normal weather outside the Puntilla Lake Lodge.

Around its wind-scoured walls, the last strands of spruce before alpine tree line, with scraggly branches all blown to one side, provided little protection. The wood stove blasted out dry heat as the lodge's manager — a teenage boy — handed me a can of clam chowder that had been boiling on a camp stove, and a thin paper napkin to hold it with. I took a plastic spoon and stirred the off-white glop around the blackened can. The soup burned my fingers and charred my throat, but I finally had some of my appetite back and did not want to waste it. I began to nibble on discs of pilot bread, a quintessential Alaska Bush emergency food that supposedly never goes soggy or stale. It tasted exactly like a soggy, stale saltine cracker.

Beds had been stacked together side by side in the tiny, single-room building. They were mostly empty now with the exception of Brij, who was sleeping soundly on a bottom bunk, and the teenager, who seemed grumpy about the necessity of staying awake past 4 a.m. He did not seem to want to chat with me.

I tried to ply information about the trail ahead and he told me simply that two guys had been up to the pass on their snowmobiles the day before, but he had no idea if the trail was broken beyond there. I asked him if any of the other cyclists had opted to go over Hell's Gate, a long-way around that veers around Rainy Pass but tacks on 33 extra miles.

He just shrugged. "I think they all went over the pass," he said.

For someone who lived so close to the edge of civilization, he didn't seem to have much interest in what existed beyond. I asked him if he stayed at the lodge year round. He said he only spent the winters there, helping out his family, who operated the lodge for hunters, snowmobilers and sled dog mushers. I smiled at the thought of a winter destination resort in Alaska. The wind outside rattled the cabin's log walls, and frost was forming near the inside corners despite the wood stove. Puntilla was a strange place to spend a winter when most Alaskans were retreating to California and Hawaii, but such is the nature of the Iditarod Trail.

I sat down on one of the beds and began to strip off my soggy clothing. I examined my problem areas and became alarmed when I saw my right knee was extremely swollen, but then again, my entire leg was swollen. I was probably just retaining water. My right big toe was surrounded in an enormous blister, which I decided I would believe was simply a blister, and not frostbite. I took three aspirin, two Tums and two glucosamine pills, covered my knees in menthol patches, popped a cough drop in my mouth and laid down on the hard mattress.

I never expected the accommodations in this race to be luxurious, but I was a bit surprised just how Spartan they actually were. People actually lived like this for entire winters. There were probably others who lived like this their entire lives, in tiny cabins set against the continent's largest mountains, with only mortared logs and wood stoves to hold back the constant needling of the fingers of death.

The unwelcome light of dawn hit my face at about 8:30 a.m. Brij was shuffling around the cabin, packing up his gear. The teenage lodge manager was still awake, and still staring blankly out the window. No one had come in behind us yet. Not Ted, and not the last straggling Euro cyclists. I half expected to see Geoff catch up to me by now, as slow as I had been moving. I looked around the room, but all the other beds were empty. I asked Brij if I could head out with him. He nodded, but we both knew I would only be able to hold his wheel for a few miles. I opted instead to take off early, let him catch me, and that way keep at least one racer in my time zone for as long as I could.

My gut was still empty when I walked into the glare of the heatless sun. I could not stomach the thought of more pilot bread and can-flavored soup. I still had a frame bag full of nuts and Clif Bars, so I certainly wasn't going to starve. The cold air wrapped around me, but its grip had been softened since the morning before. I tried to tally how many hours of sleep I had logged overnight and couldn't decide if it was three or 27. It was Tuesday now, 9 a.m., and I was already losing track of time to the relentless pull of the trail.

The morning was clear and cold and bathed in a kind of intense beauty that was nearly incapacitating, as delirious and exhausted as I was. All I could do was keep my feet on the pedals as my eyes darted around in awe. In the blindness of the night before, I had climbed all the way into the sister peaks of Mount Denali. After 165 miles of watching them from a distance, I was finally carving my way into their direct shadows.

The trail, only shallowly tracked by the two snowmobiles the lodge manager had mentioned, softened quickly in the sun. After three miles, I gave up the hard pedaling and resumed walking with my bike. A red fox darted down the trail beside me, stopping briefly to look back before it raced ahead, much faster than I could ever hope to move.

Brij soon followed, wishing me good morning as he swerved through the soft snow in his strongman effort to ride as much of the trail as possible. Sunrise climbed over the barren peaks, and the last strands of spruce gave way to thin alder branches and huge, open meadows that in the summer would be covered in tundra. In February, they were simply expanses of snow, blank sheets of paper scribbled with bare branches and the deep tracks of a dozen riders who walked through here before me.

Footprints were always a discouraging sign. Having watched them appear occasionally on the trail since the second day of the race, I had ascertained that I was one of the least skilled snow bikers out there. Most of the cyclists proved able to ride in places where I could not, and their footprints were a mark of the trail's deterioration. When there were a single set of footprints, I could often ride, but not always. When there were three or four, mine were nearly always behind them, walking. When there were eight or more, I didn't stand a chance of mounting my bike and coaxing the wheels to turn. The snow was just too soft, the incline too steep, the effort too difficult.

Still, the long bike push up into the Alaska Range was something I had expected, and nothing could sour my mood in the midst of such sweeping beauty. I pulled out my camera and shot a self portrait against the chiseled white peaks. I looked at the digital display, an image of my black hat coated in frost, a swirl of frozen hair, a bright red face and a huge smile. I looked so happy. It made me smile again.

I pulled out a celebratory peanut butter cup and stuck it in my mouth. I was becoming more used to the culinary experience of frozen food — tasteless, dry and repulsive at first bite, it would slowly dissolve into warm and creamy sustenance. It was still hard to coax much if it down. If I had a hundred peanut butter cups, I probably would have eaten them all, but I didn't, so I forced down two crunchy granola bars and called my 400-calorie breakfast good.

The wind picked up more force as the afternoon approached. I crossed the last long, open meadow and turned right into a narrow canyon, the final ascent to Rainy Pass — at 3,300 feet, the highest point on the Iditarod Trail. The trail took a turn for the very steep; the pushing became back-breaking work. I dug my boots into the snow, and with my hands clenched around the brakes, pushed the bike forward with all of my strength just so I could take another step. My shoulders ached and my biceps burned. I cursed the fact I had not spent at least some of my training time in the gym lifting big weights, but in the heatless sun of that third day, all of my physical training seemed to hardly matter anyway.

Sure, I was fit, but I had probably been nearly as fit for such an effort six months before. I really should have spent more time researching light gear, learning to ride a bike on top of soft snow, and buying peanut butter cups. It didn't even seem odd to me that, in the midst of a terribly difficult bike race, my physical fitness suddenly seemed like a moot point. Not all humans are equipped to win races, but everyone comes preprogrammed with the will to survive.

My mood swung wildly all day long. In the morning, I had experienced peaks of elation so extreme I could hardly breathe. But as I clawed my way up Rainy Pass, I found myself dipping into new depths of despair. A few times, I stopped walking because I could not visualize another step up the mountain. And then, just as it had so faithfully on Dismal Swamp in 2006, my will to survive pushed the autopilot button, and the mundane miles kept coming. After a few of those deep lows, it was hard to even pull my emotions back to normal levels. The beauty of Rainy Pass, which surrounded me like a fortress, was already slipping behind a curtain of indifference. I did not even mind the impending darkness as I crested the pass at sunset. If anything, no longer being able to see all the miles in front of me might do my emotional health some good, I thought.

I dropped down the pass several hundred yards to get out of the wind. I ducked into a rocky outcropping that was just unusual enough to have possibly been built by hands. Sure enough, I found a sign, weather faded and coated in ice, with simple black letters spelling out "Rainy Pass." I took a lot of comfort in that simple marker of civilization — proof that humans had come through there before me, and proof that I was still on the right track.

I thought wistfully of hiking with my dad as a teenager. At all of our destinations, a scenic overlook or a peak, there always seemed to be a sign or a register. We would mark our accomplishment with a phone call home and a big lunch. But there, on the wind-swept ice of Rainy Pass, there was no cell phone reception for miles. I rifled through my frame bag to look for something to eat for lunch and realized that the setting sun meant it was nearly 6 p.m. I had eaten next to nothing since my granola bar and peanut butter cup breakfast— a few nuts here and there, a few dried cranberries and fruit leathers. I was probably lucky if I had a thousand calories in me for the entire day, and still I did not feel hungry. I settled on two more peanut butter cups — even though I already had eaten my daily allotment — half of a five-ounce chocolate bar, and a Clif Bar that I had been thawing in my coat pocket. It was a meager dinner and it tasted like frozen mud, but it was my duty as a survivor to put it down.

As I started down the pass, the footprints grew more deep and even more numerous. In fact, all I could see were footprints. There were no longer any snowmobile tracks, no evidence of any trail at all. There were simply the racers who came before me, stomping through knee-deep snow down the steep slope, laying the only path I had to follow as night descended. After three more miles of slow downhill walking and no evidence of any trail at all, it became apparent that not only did I have to walk up Rainy Pass, I was going to have to walk down it as well.

Downhill pushing was an effort I never anticipated. With big tires, bicycle riding in the snow is nearly always possible downhill, even when the trail is soft. But without a tracked trail, weight just sinks into the powder and wheels become useless. A set of skis or snowshoes could have at least offered my body some float, but I had none.

I waded through the knee-deep snow and wondered aloud, to the peaks disappearing into the night above me, how much farther it was to the next checkpoint, Rohn. I guessed it was at least 20 miles. At my most hopeful walking speed, 2 mph, I still had 10 more hours to push. In the midst of a powder slog, my pace was probably closer to 1 mph. The need for sleep was surrounding me like a smothering cocoon. I did not know if I could handle another all-nighter, but did not believe I could survive a night out.

So I walked, because walking meant life, and stopping meant death, and in that state of extremes, there is actually little to fear. I knew I had to keep moving, so I did. All of the surrounding threats — the cold, the moose and wolves, the open streams, the looming darkness, the remote location — faded behind a primal drive to stay in motion. Although I was quickly succumbing to exhaustion and becoming more aware of just how far I had still to go, I did not despair. I did not even hit the same level of lows that I had experienced mere hours earlier, when my toughest challenge was pushing my bike up a steep hill. I felt good, actually, because I was still moving. And as long as I was moving, I was alive.

Several hours passed into oblivion, not quite awake but not yet asleep, as my bobbing light cast a sickly yellow glow on the endless march of footprints. I followed them, down steep hills, beside the twisting branches of spruce trees, across thin ice over a rushing stream and into the heart of the night's darkness. I was lucky to have those footprints. If it had been up to me to navigate myself in that state of mind, I might have walked right off a cliff or into open water. But it's hard to say how inept I would have been if I had been completely on my own. The will to survive is strong, and it drives as effectively as it can, but only as much as it has to.

In countless hours of post-race reflection, I have tried to piece together the sequence of "what went wrong" in those final hours awake on the backside of Rainy Pass. My memories are dim at best, obscured by physical overload and mounting indifference. But I remember stopping, the way I had dozens of times that day, turning off my headlamp and looking up at the sky. A dim ribbon of green light wavered in the narrow strip of sky above the mountains, peaks so white they glowed against the moonless night. Stars glistened behind the northern lights, and I groped for the elation I deserved, the appropriate response to unspeakable beauty. I felt nothing. I turned on my light and moved to take a step, but my legs wouldn't move. They simply refused to move. I knelt into the snow and let out a long, almost relieved sigh.

My will to survive was firing just enough to alert my retreated intelligence that I was in the midst of a serious bonk. I had run out of fuel, finally and completely. The will to survive would have let me continue if I had no other choice, but what little intelligence I had left reminded me that I did have other choices. I had pushed my body to a state of inescapable exhaustion, but I had come prepared for the possibility of motionlessness.

My bike still held survival sleeping gear — stuff I had only used and tested a handful of times. So it was strange that like clockwork, like a routine I had practiced a hundred times, I unhooked my bivy bundle, dug a deep trench in the snow, threw a few spruce branches in the hole, unrolled my bivy and crawled inside.

My body warmth filled the sack and I took several deep breaths while comforting myself with out-loud exclamations that "this isn't that bad." I reached out to pull my CamelBak, my only source of water, inside with me, and cuddled with the frigid bladder of half-frozen water.

Knowing I was in the midst of a bonk mandated as much food as I could stomach, but I was only able to put down the other half of my chocolate bar from dinner. At least I was warm, warm enough to let the fear encompass me again, and the quick glance at my thermometer, still bottomed out at 20 below after two minutes inside my bag, was enough to reignite my smoldering fear. What if the warm cocoon surrounding me failed? How would I possibly crawl 10 or more miles into Rohn? I heard a low, dull howl in the distance that was either a wolf or the wind. I could not remember the last time I felt so alone.

Buckskin Gulch, Utah
May 2001

The frost coating my sleeping bag in the morning set off all kinds of new alarms in my mind.

The first light of dawn glowed pink over sandstone cliffs, casting an ominously cool glow over the surrounding desert. I nudged Geoff, who was wrapped inside his own icy bag next to me in the sand.

"Geoff," I hissed. "Wake up! Everything's frozen!"

Geoff kicked from inside his cocoon and peeked out of a small opening near his head. "Huh?"

There's frost everywhere! My sleeping bag is frozen!" I said.

"So?"

"So," I said. "We can't possibly hike Buckskin Gulch in this kind of weather. We'll freeze. We'll die."

Buckskin Gulch is a narrow slot canyon straddling the Utah and Arizona borders. At that time of year, early May, the canyon was sure to be full of pooled water that had never seen the sun.

"We'll be fine," Geoff said. He sat up and looked around. "This is a good thing. Oh, don't worry. It will warm up. At least it won't be wicked hot."

Our friends Jamie and Jen were already stirring from their respective hovels. Jamie crawled out from the back seat of the car as Jen thrashed around in her sleeping bag.

"Well, this sucks ass," Jen said after she finally wrestled her way free and emerged in our frozen world.

"We're in the desert. It gets cold at night," Geoff said, exasperated, as he stuffed his sleeping bag into his backpack. "Don't act like it's the end of the world."

"We're going to die," Jen said. "Yeah, we're going to die."

"How much water do you think there is in Buckskin Gulch?" Jamie said in her quiet, earnest way.

She was smiling, but there were flecks of fear in her voice that made me feel that much worse. Jamie and Jen had plenty of experience in Southern Utah canyoneering. I, on the other hand, had spent my teenage years sticking to the straightforward trails of national parks and peaks near Salt Lake City. If Jamie was scared, where did that leave me?

"I don't know," Geoff said. "There are probably a few bigger pools in there. Shouldn't be anything over our heads. I don't think it ever gets that deep."

"Oh, that's reassuring," I said. "So at least we won't have to swim before we get hypothermia."

"No one's getting hypothermia," Geoff said. "But we should get going soon if we want to make it through to the camp spot tonight. We still have a ways to drive."

About an hour and a half down the road, we reached the trailhead at the end of a rough dirt track. Geoff, Jamie, Jen and I filtered out of the car and hoisted our backpacks. The sun was out in full force, but it was by no means warm. I had anticipated sloshing through cold pools of water, but it never occurred to me to prepare differently for it than I would for any other hike. I was wearing a pair of old jeans, a cotton T-shirt, a polar fleece vest, and a pair of shoes that were three sizes too big. They were borrowed old running shoes from Geoff. I did not want to get my good hiking shoes wet.

I had one change of clothes in my pack — another pair of jeans and a cotton shirt — as well as a little food, water and my frosty sleeping bag. My full-sized sleeping pad was tied to the outside of my backpack. Geoff and I had opted to bring a tarp instead of a tent. It was lighter, he reasoned, and we were in the desert. What chance did we have of being rained on?

Jen didn't even bring a change of clothing. She had an old down coat held together by a patchwork of duct tape. Jamie and Geoff were more realistic, and were both outfitted with nylon pants and water resistant jackets. None of us had ever been down the long, narrow slot canyon that empties into the Paria River — storied, photogenic, and incredibly remote.

The sandy wash wove through sun-streaked shadows of sandstone fins, then quickly descended into the bowels of the ever-shaded canyon. Mere feet to either side of our shoulders, sheer sandstone towers stretched toward a thin slit of blue sky. The wash became deeper and cooler with every step. The canyon walls were marbled with distinct layers of rock — glistening whites etching stark lines between muted orange, brick red and charcoal black hues. The rock was so smooth I could run my fingers along the surface and find no handholds to grab; the walls were so close together I could reach out with both arms and touch both sides. The skeletons of pinion trees, washed in by past flash floods, were wedged between slabs of stone dozens of feet above our heads. It was beautiful, but in an apprehensive way. It seemed like we were descending into an inescapable cage.

After about two miles, we arrived at our first point of no return: a 10-foot sheer drop that required a direct leap to descend. Without a rope, there was no way to climb out. Once we dropped in, we were committed until the canyon's end. We threw our packs to the sand and jumped. Even Geoff acknowledged that "this is it."

My old fears kicked up as I flew through the air, but began to settle nicely as I dusted myself off and picked up my pack. I sauntered through ankle-deep pools of black water in my humongous shoes and jeans as my lumbering, ill-fitted backpack swayed over my head. I felt like a professional backpacker, and it wasn't too bad of a place to be.

Buckskin Gulch qualified as my first serious backpack trip, with the exception of a backcountry class I took at the university that hardly counted, and an overnight camping trip I once went on with an ex-boyfriend in which I carried a sleeping-bag stuffed book bag and a pillow tied with a rope to the outside. Buckskin Gulch was my first excursion into self-supported wilderness adventure. Two miles in, and I couldn't think of any reason why I wasn't every bit as fit and prepared as any old pro.

And just as I settled in to my comfortable stride, a high-volume obscenity echoed through the canyon.

"What? What is it?" Geoff called out as we rounded a sharp bend in the canyon. Jen was standing at the edge of a foul-smelling pool, the color of rancid chocolate milk and coated in beige froth.

"I can't even see the end of this one," Jen said. "It's like it goes on forever."

"Well, let's get this over with," Geoff said. He plunged in first and sloshed through the noxious water as it rippled around his knees. I knelt down and stuck my fingers in the pool. It was as cold as any mountain stream I had ever walked through, but sickly stagnant. I tenderly stepped in and inhaled sharply as the frigid water sucked all the body heat right out of my shins. Geoff rounded the next corner as I followed. We came to another tight bend, and another, and still as far as I could see, there was no end to the water.

"Can't you move any faster?" Jen said directly behind me. "This is really cold."

"I don't want to trip," I said, as my flipper-like shoes vacuumed up large quantities of water with every step. I flattened my back against one canyon wall and let her squeeze by. Jamie followed, stoically and wordlessly. I brought up the rear.

Instead of drying up, the snaking pool only became deeper. The soup-thick water crept up to my waist and then my stomach. I had to hoist my backpack to keep the fabric from soaking up silt water and sludge. My sleeping pad scraped ominously against the rock walls, which were now barely wider than my backpack. Every ripping sound reminded me that my air mattress was being shredded. But I had no place to take off my backpack and rearrange my gear, so I accepted it as the canyon's first casualty. More concerning was the fact that I could no longer feel any sensation in my legs. I could only hope the water level would not rise above my heart.

I caught up to Jen, who was trying in vain to hold the bottom of her down coat above the water line. She was shivering violently. "Do you think we should turn back?" she said.

"We can't," I said. "Remember that cliff we jumped down?"

"How much longer do you think this pool goes?" Jen said. "I have to get out of here."

"I don't know," I said. I felt as bewildered as she looked, although grateful that I wasn't as visibly cold. We continued forward in relative silence, interrupted by Jen's occasional, unanswered questions — "Is that the end? Does that look like the end?"

We met two other hikers who were wearing wet suits and small packs. The told us they were taking a day hike up from Paria Canyon. We asked them if they could offer us any hope. "It's only about another half mile," one of the men said.

Another. Half. Mile? We had already walked at least a half mile in the knee-to-waist-deep pool, and even that seemed like an eternity. Still, the prospect of any end at all brightened our spirits. But a half hour later, when we were certain that endless half mile must have passed, and we were still slogging through the water, Jen was quiet and pale. I thought she might start to cry. Later, she would tell us she was moderately hypothermic and fighting for consciousness.

It wasn't much farther, another 100 yards, when we finally saw our first solid patch of ground in more than an hour. Jamie and Geoff were waiting for us. They had changed into their set of dry clothes. Jen finally admitted she had nothing to change into, and I wasn't willing to change into my only replacements until I knew the pools were done.

"That was unbelievably awful," I said.

"It wasn't that bad," Geoff said.

"It was chest deep!" I cried.

"It wasn't that deep," he said, so I lifted up my fleece vest to reveal my white cotton shirt, marked with a dark brown ring all the way to my collar.

Jen announced she couldn't stop shivering. We hobbled over a small patch of sunlight on the canyon floor and tried to coax jumping jacks out of our cold muscles until shadows crept over the light.

"It's getting a little cloudy," Geoff said. "We should start moving."

Sure enough, the blue slit of sky darkened to a pale shade of gray, and then a dark shade of gray. We heard a few low rumbles, and then drops of water began to trickle down the sheer canyon walls.

"It's raining!" I yelled, to no one, really. Everyone knew it was raining. And everyone knew what that meant. In a slot canyon, in the desert, rain can only mean one thing: the flash flood alert meter moves into the red.

"We'll be fine," Geoff said. "Just keep moving."

I couldn't tell if he was becoming nervous, but I found the sprinkles of water from the sky more terrifying than miles of rancid, frigid pools. Very quickly, the sprinkles turned to sheets of rain, and then real waterfalls started cascading from the plateau hundreds of feet above our heads. Around our feet, streams started to form and flow. It seemed like mere minutes before the water was already around our ankles.

"The canyon is filling with water!" Jamie yelled. It was her first real statement of fear. Jen was very quiet again. Geoff informed us we should probably start running.

He and Jen took off quickly. Geoff had natural power, and Jen was probably in deep survival mode. But my legs, which were just starting to come back from the numbing cold, refused to pick up the pace. My jeans were soaked and stiff against my legs, radiating all of the heat my body's furnace could afford to kick out, until my slowly warming skin felt like it was on fire. My huge shoes sloshed and stuck to the mud. I felt like a clown, and every effort I made to move quickly was morbidly comical, like a fall-down drunk person plodding through a blizzard.

Jamie stayed with me for a bit, probably out of concern, but even she began to put some distance on me. Every time I heard the faintest roar, my heart leapt into my lungs. The flash flood was coming, I thought. I certainly needed high ground. I thought about taking off my shoes and pants, dropping my pack, and just bolting. I looked around the canyon and made note of the grottos I could duck into and the debris I could cling to when the floods did come.

For some unknown reason, my fear had hit a state of arrested development — just before the fever pitch sent me into a panic, but not in time to keep me from slipping into the indifference that comes with perceived doom. I could not accept what I was certain was my impending death by drowning, but I couldn't run from it either. So I just walked.

I walked beside the dark brown waterfalls that gushed from the lips of the plateau. I walked past veins of ancient rock and through now-shin-deep streams that hours before had been dry sand. I did not see the beauty and I did not think about the future. Only the steps, every step, each one hopeful with the possibility of being the step that would finally carry me to safety; or, likewise, fearful of being the last step I ever made.

So it was almost with disbelief that I walked into a large, open grotto with a sandy bluff to one side. It was surrounded by tamarisk bushes and a couple of cottonwood trees that looked to have survived several decades of flash floods. Up on the bluff, I could see Geoff working on building a tarp shelter. He was 40, maybe 50 feet above the canyon floor — tall enough to shelter us from all but the worst flash floods, should one even come. I darted up the steep slope, my heart starting to race now that the impending doom had passed, and I could finally enjoy a delayed surge of adrenaline.

"We lived!" I announced. "We're alive."

I rifled through my backpack until I found the one thing that mattered now, and tore open the plastic bag that held the pound of cheese I had packed in.

"That's for the burritos!" Geoff yelled as he saw me gnawing on the brick of cheddar like a greedy rat.

Jamie walked up and asked for a bite, so I broke of a large chunk for her. Then Jen joined in. The pain and cold faded into a warm feeling of satisfaction. And deep in the canyon, where danger lurked in every corner behind us, gratification was instant. Geoff, seeing three somewhat hypothermic and sincerely frightened girls devouring his only chance of high-fat sustenance, finally walked up and collected his share.

"The burritos will be gross without this," he said.

"Screw the burritos," Jen said, polishing off the last of her four ounces. I felt like I had just been shown the secret key to turning fear into joy.

Dalzell Gorge, Alaska
February 27, 2008

Warm air swirled around my face when I opened my eyes, which surprised me, because I immediately remembered where I was.

A thick humidity filled the darkness inside my sleeping bag. My breaths were still short and frequent. What time was it? How long had I been asleep? Had I been asleep? Or did I just lose consciousness for a few minutes before jolting back awake again? I pulled my legs toward my chest and grabbed my feet, which felt numb. The thick wool socks were coated in some kind of sharp, cold layer. Frost? Could that be frost?

I began to hyperventilate again and groped around the assortment of gear near my head until I found my headlamp. I turned it on and pointed it at my feet as I ripped the socks away from my skin. I expected to find black blisters wrapped around my toes, but in the soft light, everything looked normal. I willed my toes to wiggle and they did, just like they always had. I wrapped by fingers around them and they felt icy cold in my hands, but they were moving, they were in tact, and I was alive. I was alive! I don't know what else I had expected, but the realization of this simple fact gave me a new boost of confidence.

I glanced at my watch. It was 4:30 in the morning. Wednesday. I hadn't looked at my watch before I laid down, but I guessed I had slept for three or four hours.

I felt like a flu-ridden child trying to pry myself awake from a fever nap. An adrenaline surge from the frozen feet scare still coursed through my veins, and I knew I either had to reach away from my exhaustion or spend another feverish few hours drifting in and out of consciousness in my bag. My feet throbbed and burned as they began the familiar rewarming process, and I recognized the possibility that I only woke up in the first place because frostbite really was setting in. I opted to start moving.

I kicked out of my bag, squeezed into my frozen boots and frantically danced around my bivy spot in the dark, trying to fend off the sharp assault of cold air. I knew I faced a few unbearably cold minutes of down time while I packed up my gear before I could start riding and rewarming my extremities, so I sprinted up and down the trail until I no longer had the energy to run. Then I knelt into the snow, removed my mittens and and began the methodical process of rolling up my bivy sack and buckling it into its bundle.

The cold stabbed at my fingers but packing was exponentially faster without mittens, so I clenched my teeth and bared it until I could no longer move my fingers. Then I pulled my mittens on, wrapped my fingers around a lukewarm chemical warmer, did jumping jacks until they came back to life, and started the process again.

The frequently interrupted packing took about 20 minutes to complete, and I celebrated both my success and my survival with one of the day's peanut butter cups and a few stiff handfuls of dried cranberries. I mounted my bike and rode a few hundred feet as my rear wheel dug deeper and deeper into the snow until it stopped moving all together. The trail was still every bit as soft as it had been the night before. I hopped off and resumed the trudge. Some of my steps sunk all the way to my knees. I started stepping only in the tracks of others and rolling my bike over their tire marks, which required me to move my bike from my left side to my right side. The new position felt strange. The footprints were so deep that my handlebars hovered near my neckline, and every step into the dark postholes became an ankle-twisting leap of faith.

My bike creaked and groaned as I dragged it beside me. Often the bike became tangled in branches and I would stop to wrestle it out. Many other times, I lost my balance in deeper-than-expected holes. Whenever I came to a big snow drift, I had to stop and lift the bike over my shoulder. Every time the wheels had to come off the ground, the effort added an exponential exhaustion factor to each step. I couldn't believe how tired I felt.

In my swirling thoughts of doubt and fear, I tried to reason ways I could somehow recover from that night and stay in the race. But I was already comprehending all the ways in which my race was over. I thought briefly of all the people who would be disappointed, the friends and family, the strangers who had sent donations and cards, the people in their warm houses who were glued to Internet updates, just as I had been a year earlier. I knew they were out there, watching for me right at that moment. The thought of quitting broke my heart — quitting my dream, my race.

"This is a long race," I chanted out loud. "A long race, and there's still time."

But another voice, a louder voice, crept up from my frozen toes, my empty gut and worn-out heart.

"This isn't a race," the voice from the ghost of my past said. "This is your life."

After a couple of slow miles, the footprints stopped dead at the edge of a rushing stream. I nearly pushed right through it before my stifled intelligence wrestled its way through the indifference of fatigue.

That was open water, and the temperature was at least 20 below zero. Anything that became wet would freeze within seconds of being re-exposed to the air. Wet feet — almost a given in all of my training in the soggy climes of Juneau — were not an option this time.

I started to hyperventilate again, but the fact remained there were footprints on that side of the stream and footprints on the other side of the stream, and there weren't dead bodies strewn everywhere. Others had conquered that obstacle. I put down my bike and followed the footprints as they backtracked and broke through the steep banks toward an open spot upstream. From there, a crossing much more narrow but extremely deep came into view. It looked like the strongmen had jumped from one side to the other. But how did they do it with their bikes? It was too far to leap with that much extra weight, too risky. The landing was on a slanted slope, and tossing my bike, even if it successfully spanned the gap, would likely result in it sliding back into the open water. I could only guess that most of the strongmen had crossed it with another person, and handed their bikes carefully over the deadly gap.

I, however, was completely alone, and I hadn't seen another human since Brij passed me on his bike nearly 24 hours earlier. I was either going to have to cross the small stream or turn around, and I couldn't fathom the thought of turning around. The stream was another obstacle among hundreds, and I just wanted to get it over with. I had prepared for the contingency of open water, unlikely as I hoped it would be, by packing two large heavy-duty garbage bags. I pulled them over my legs and haphazardly wrapped duct table around my thighs, realizing I left large open holes where the plastic clumped up but not believing that to be a problem. The water didn't look that deep. I hoisted my bike onto my shoulder — it felt like I was trying to move a piano — and stepped into the stream.

The rush of current startled me and immediately knocked me off balance. I wavered and tried to step backward onto the bank, but it was too late. I could feel my heavy bike slipping out of my hands. My heart raced. My stomach lurched. I leaned against the pull gravity and strained to keep my body upright. I heard a sickening splash and instinctively whirled around to grab the bicycle I had just dropped directly into the water.

As I knelt in to grab the top tube of the frame, a surge of cold water rushed into the garbage bag around my right leg. The water soaked through my pants and filled my boot, instantly sapping my lower body of all of its heat. I gasped at the sudden shock of sensation, like being struck by a bullet in the midst of an anesthesia fog.

The damage had been done so I knelt in deeper to gain a good grip on my half-tipped bike, managing to save the frame from falling completely over and soaking all of my gear, but failing to keep the wheels and drivetrain out of the water. Those parts would soon freeze solid, unable to roll or shift gears, but the bigger concern was the water in my boot.

I marched through the depths of the stream and crawled out on the other side, gasping for breath as I tossed the bike in the snow and tore the garbage bags off my legs. I had managed to keep my left leg dry, but the outer shell on my right leg was already ringed in frost. My boot was soaked. I felt like a complete idiot — a doomed idiot.

"Don't panic, don't panic, don't panic," I chanted out loud through sharp breaths.

My options seemed dire, and yet my will to survive forced me to sit there, struggling to breathe normally and give serious consideration to every one. Should I crawl into my bivy and wait for help? No, I wasn't injured, yet. And who knew how fast help would even come? And how would I explain that I wanted to be rescued because my foot was wet? And how ashamed would I feel if it turned out to be Geoff who found me? No, I would have to get myself out of this idiotic situation.

Should I just ignore my wet foot and continue walking? I decided I could stay mindful and continue to wiggle my toes, and if they stopped wiggling, I would remove my wet boot and wrap my right foot in all of the extra layers and chemical warmers I had, tape a garbage bag around it, and limp into camp. Through the darkness and fatigue of the morning, that seemed like a perfectly reasonable option. I didn't like to think about the garbage bag part, so I resolved to wiggle my toes constantly. The only thing I was sure of was that my race was over. And all that mattered at the point was getting to Rohn.

The sun came up some hours later, and I still had a long way to march. My foot, despite being wet, had retained a normal temperature thanks to the constant walking, which became even more difficult as the canyon grew deeper and the footprints more uneven. The strongmen probably thought they had it hard, breaking trail, but their tracks were also incredibly difficult to follow. Eventually, I started breaking my own trail a few inches to the side of their path.

All around me, the new dawn gave depth to the surroundings I had been struggling with during a seemingly eternal night. I noticed I was skimming the sideslope of a deep, narrow canyon. The surrounding mountains shut out the light and gave the river gorge the claustrophobic feel of a slot canyon in the desert. The stream I had soaked my foot in hours before had dropped hundreds of feet below the trail. Open water rushed beneath a porous shell of ice, quickly making its way toward the Tatina River. I glanced at my GPS and noticed the river wasn't far from there — a few miles at the most. But at the pace I was moving, that was a few hours. I wondered if I had ever before experienced something so excruciatingly slow.

Despite my frustration, I could still look through the hopelessness and see the canyon for the stunning beauty it harbored, hidden away from almost everybody else in this harsh, uninhabited part of the world. Chiseled cliffs descended into a thick spruce forest, which obscured the snaking stream and its partly-frozen rapids. The trail took a few hairpin turns into the depths of the canyon. I watched the emerging sunlight cast streaks of color across slopes high above my head. The trail continued down canyon until I was standing directly over the creek. A few crossings were nothing more than ice bridges over open water. My heart stopped beating as I crossed them, but below my feet they glistened blue and white like crystal sculptures, beautiful works of art born of raw inspiration and natural rage.

When I emerged on the Tatina River, I had calmed down quite a bit. The certainty that I had just tangled with death became more vague as I assessed what really happened that night. I did not run out of calories, keel over, and simply die. I just felt a little tired so I laid down to rest, got a little food in me, and got back up. My foot did not flash freeze. It got wet, but my warm-blooded body was an efficient system after all, and nothing bad came of a little splashing through the cold water.

All of the despair and doom of Rainy Pass faded into the background as I mounted my bike on the flat, smooth river and pedaled toward the open sunlight, the end of the canyon, and the Unknown that was Alaska's Interior. The wheels shed their coating of ice as I rode, but, as expected, the bike's drivetrain was stuck in place. Both derailleurs were frozen solid and every effort to chip away the ice and unjam the shifters would not make them move. I was singlespeeding, and likely would remain stuck in a single speed for the remainder of the race, whether it went five more miles or 150.

"Oh well," I said to my frozen, creaking bike. "At least you're stuck in granny gear." I no longer was certain about quitting. But I remained convinced that the worst of the race still lay ahead, in the ice box of the Interior.

The sunlight of 10 a.m. felt almost warm as I neared the Kuskokwim River, the same river that flowed out of the Alaska Range and all of the way into McGrath. Those who didn't understand the nature of this race would believe it was all downhill from there, but I knew better. I knew the trail abandoned the river and climbed back into the hills before dropping into the wildfire-charred wasteland known only abstractly as the Farewell Burn. All of these places scared me, buried as they were in the sun shadow of the Alaska Range, where temperatures could be and usually were 20 to 30 degrees colder than the air on the other side of the mountains. Blizzards could and usually did strike without warning. Snow usually fell in flakes as hard and dry as fine grain sugar, the kind of snow that never set up and was impossible to ride on top of. Wolves prowled and ravens shrieked. Nobody else lived out there. Out there was the heart of darkness. Rainy Pass was a walk in the park.

I walked the last mile of woods before emerging on an airplane landing strip lined with straw bales and huge bags of dog food. The Iditarod Trail Dog Sled Race would start in less than a week, and it seemed strange that such a quiet and scary place was days away from becoming a circus of human volunteers and hordes of sled dogs.

Humans have accomplished some amazing things, but the fact they could inject civilization into this uninhabitable wilderness seemed like the most amazing accomplishment of all. I snapped a quick celebratory picture by an Iditarod Trail sign before I went to rejoin the now-foreign circus of civilization myself.

Mount Borah, Idaho
July 14, 2001

In the dust-infused light of a windy afternoon, I was sure I had misread the sign at the trailhead.

"Fifty two hundred feet?" I said as Geoff closed the door of my dust-coated car and joined me at the base of the mountain. "The elevation gain is 5,200? Feet? In three and a quarter miles? How does that even work? Are there ropes and ladders up there or something?"

I glanced toward the jagged ridge where it sliced into the hazy sky. Giant slabs of rock shimmered in the afternoon sun. Beyond the ridge was the peak I had watched from a long distance north. Now too near to see, that peak had been the one thing that dominated the skyline amid miles of lava rocks and sagebrush fields — Mount Borah, the tallest mountain in Idaho.

I looked at Geoff and frowned. We had already driven several hundred miles that day, all the way from an arbitrary camp spot somewhere in central Montana. It was just one among dozens of arbitrary camp spots that we peppered the continent with as we drove thousands of miles during a summer-long road trip. We had busted out another long stretch of driving on a Friday morning, watching Idaho's high point grow larger by the mile. When Geoff suggested we climb it, I reluctantly acknowledged that we probably should because I might never get another chance to bag that particular peak. I sometimes dreamed about striving for the goal of summitting each of the high points in all 50 states. Idaho, if I made it, would be my first.

The time was well beyond noon, and the hot July sun beat down through the dirty, cloudless sky. I was road-weary and battling with the perpetual drowsiness of life on the move. Just moments before I had been drifting in and out of sleep as Geoff drove my road-weary car across the plains of eastern Idaho. The pull of home, less than one day's drive south, was stronger than ever, and I was unsure what sounded more appealing and what sounded more painful — the marathon drive toward my own bed, or the marathon climb up Mount Borah.

"It's just three miles," Geoff said. "Yeah, it's a lot of climbing, but this is a big, popular trail. It shouldn't be that hard." He looked at his watch. "1:30. We should have plenty of time."

"It says right here that hikers should start at dawn," I said, pointing to the trail head sign. "Oh, and here ... 'death' ... 'falling risk' ... 'exposure' ... yup, sounds easy." I analyzed every line of text, cracked and faded by harsh winters and harsher sun. Why were forest service officials so insistent on advertising only the danger of trails? There wasn't anything on the sign about stunning views or clear mountain streams stocked with gold. I was far from sold.

"Since when are those signs ever right?" Geoff said. "They're just trying to keep people away that don't know what they're doing." I gestured toward myself as he said it. Geoff pretended not to notice. "So do you want to go or not?"

"I suppose," I said as I let out a long sigh. "I guess we'll just see how far we can get."

I took my first steps lazily, but the Mount Borah trail didn't dawdle, even for a second. Before the trailhead sign was even out of view, Geoff and I were scrambling up a 45-degree slope coated with sharp lava rocks and lined with the fire-charred skeletons of pinion trees. My heart rate skyrocketed and the veins in my wrists started to throb. The heat of the sun radiated off the mountain, and I struggled to even see where I was going through streams of sweat that were gushing down my forehead. I dropped to my hands and started feeling my way up the prickly trail. The lava rocks seared my palms, hot enough to convince me that they were either radioactive or the deposits of a recent volcano blast. I eventually had to pull my hands away.

Geoff quickly climbed a good distance ahead and I let him go. We had learned over the course of our two-month trip that we were happiest when we moved at our own pace, reconvening when it made sense. During any hard effort, Geoff and I thrived best in solitude. Geoff thrived at pushing his strengths when there was no one to hold him back. I thrived at overcoming my weaknesses when there was no one to criticize my efforts. And at the base of Borah, already locked in one of my deepest levels of personal struggle, I was grateful Geoff wasn't around.

Soon my labored steps took on a mindless rhythm ... the kick, kick into the loose scree, the tumble of uprooted pebbles, the white noise of the wind and my own heavy breaths that punctuated the harmony. The highway we had driven in on stretched out in the distance, a string of pavement becoming thinner every time I looked back. I wondered if I even knew the name or number of that highway, or if I could remember anything about the tiny towns strung along it. Every secondary highway in America seemed to have that similar look and feel — a ribbon of order amid a great void.

But my life looked remarkably different from the new perspective that a summer on the road had afforded me. At least I wanted to believe it looked different, that I had learned something invaluable from the North American continent that I could bring back to my routine life. It had only been two months since Geoff and I quit our jobs, moved out of our apartments, picked up the remaining pieces of our home-based lives and packed up my car for a meandering trip toward destination unknown.

It was a cross-country road trip in the classic sense of the term, but beyond that, it was my and Geoff's first real date — a roving experiment in compatibility and cooperation. We headed south from Salt Lake City and backpacked the length of Zion National Park. We pitched our tent over the white sands of New Mexico and ate grilled-cheese sandwiches amid the bobbing oil drills of west Texas. We stormed through the south, living in free campgrounds amid the bugs and the bayous, before snaking up the Eastern Seaboard to Geoff's hometown in upstate New York. From there we explored the northeast, Quebec, Ontario and finally Minnesota and Montana as we descended back toward home. We were so close to Salt Lake that I could already feel the pull of my once-routine lifestyle. The stress about finding a new job and a new place to live seemed to blot out everything I had learned about being carefree and broke. And as hard as it was to face the miles to Mount Borah, I started to feel worse about facing the last miles of our trip.

My head was spinning by the time I passed the last bristly bushes below tree line. I was amazed how little distance I had covered. I could still see the highway when I looked behind me, still less than a mile away as the bird flies. But the vertical rise was crushing. Geoff sat at the base of a saddle, munching on a Power Bar as he patiently waited for me to shuffle toward him.

I momentarily made eye contact, but soon couldn't pull my gaze away from what lie beyond him. A knife-sharp spine shot thousands of feet higher before curving like a dragon's neck toward what had to be the peak. To each side of the spine were near-vertical scree fields that almost certainly would punish even small missteps with a deadly tumble. I couldn't recall ever seeing a mountain ridge so narrow or exposed, and there I was, trying to climb one.

"I really don't feel great," I announced as I sat down beside him. He offered me a bite of his crumpled Power Bar and I shook my head. "I think it might be the elevation or something. I have a headache and I feel like I'm going to throw up. I'm not sure why. Probably because I'm not used to the elevation. What are we at? 11,000 feet?"

"More like 10,000 here," Geoff said. "It's still a long way to the top."

"Right," I said. "And I'm already slowing down."

"So do you think we should go back?" Geoff asked.

I looked into Geoff's eyes. Something told me he genuinely didn't care one way or the other. For Geoff, adventure — like physical fitness — came naturally, so it really didn't matter whether he trekked to the top of the tallest peak in Idaho, or simply laid down in the sand beneath the mountain's shadow and let the afternoon unravel slowly. He was happy either way. I, on the other hand, had started out miserable and was becoming progressively worse.

But I did care. We had come that far, and I could already feel a cool mountain breeze easing some of the sweat and struggle, so I told him I wanted to go on.

Geoff resumed his pace up the ridge. I quickly found myself alone again amid the boulders, swinging my legs over steep pitches and kneeling on narrow perches as I searched for foolproof handholds. The route demanded full-on scrambling, and we hadn't even reached the exposed section yet. I truly felt sick to my stomach, and I suspected it had nothing to do with elevation.

I was still uncertain how I felt about Geoff coaxing me so far out of my comfort zone. After I returned from my New York vacation at the beginning of 2001, I took a job at a suburban weekly newspaper that folded six weeks later. I lost out on three weeks pay, bounced a dozen of my own checks, and experienced an emotional breakdown amid the financial disorder. I quickly signed up for a graphic design job that I did not fit well and did not like. In those first months of my post-college adulthood, I could see the scope of my workaday future in all of its mundane chaos. And all the while, I had Geoff urging me to give it all up, to free myself of my possessions and my bills, and live my life in the moment, day by day.

I quit my job in May and hit the road with him. He promised to show me the ways in which he found freedom in poverty. He wanted to teach me that time was life's most valuable currency, and the duration of it was most valuably spent on the move. We braided hemp necklaces we hoped to sell for gas money, expended a lot of energy searching for places to sleep and things to eat, and whatever time we had left, we spent hiking.

By July, my muscles were toned and my skin was bronzed, but my mind was tired. Even as we bathed in the remote beauty of the Blue Ridge Mountains or a nameless lake in Maine, I started to think often about our brief brushes with civilization.

In June, we made a three-day detour to a massive arena in Camden, New Jersey, to sell our jewelry. The idea was the make enough money to pay for our trip, to buy the time we had so joyfully spent. Huge crowds packed the parking lot to sit near their cars and drink large quantities of beer ahead of a series of Dave Matthews concerts. We walked among them, holding out our jewelry bundles and calling out "Hemp jewelry, five dollars!"

I had been on the receiving end of that same scene at least a dozen times as a teenager, but it didn't occur to me what my place in the world had become until a teenage girl wearing designer jeans sprinted toward me yelling "Hippy Lady! Hippy Lady!" It took me a moment to realize that I was the one she was calling Hippy Lady. This girl, who just a few years earlier I would have considered my peer, was calling me Hippy Lady. I became startlingly self conscious of my ratty hair, my ripped cargo pants, my sun-faded T-shirt and scuffed hiking shoes. I was a dirty hippy with a handful of hemp that was my only source of income. The girl bought $70 worth of jewelry from me without even blinking. I wanted to tell her that it meant nearly a week of gas and food, but even I could hardly comprehend the chasm between us — the difference of how much that money meant to me versus how little it meant to her. I knew then that the joys of poverty only stretched as far as a full stomach and a warm place to sleep, and I wasn't even guaranteed those things as I woke up each beautiful morning and headed down the road. As much as I had seen with Geoff, I couldn't help but long for my less humble beginnings.

The air had turned crisp, almost fall-like, as the ridge leveled out and I had a full view of the ominous bumps of Borah's backbone. Geoff had waited for me again at a place where the neck made its first fatal dip toward the bowl, and I motioned for him to keep moving because I did not want him to see me shaking. I would later learn this section of the mountain is called "Chicken Out Ridge," and it took every ounce of strength I had left to not. I wrapped both arms around a boulder and looked around, the hazy sky clearing, the jagged mountains rippling toward the distant horizon, and below us, far below us, there was still the highway, stretching forever farther.

My vision was beginning to blur again, and I could not reconcile the beauty of the vista with the darkness in my heart. At moments like these, it was easy to be mad at Geoff, to blame him somehow, even though every decision I made had been my own. When we drove through Arcadia National Park in Maine, I wanted to go hiking and he didn't. So I set out alone. Halfway through my hike, a sleeping woman's pet pit bull lunged at me and latched onto my leg, leaving two bleeding puncture wounds on my thigh. I jogged, sobbing uncontrollably, all the way back to my car, where Geoff was waiting for me. As he tried to calm me down, I was seething about his absence. I could hardly talk to him through my anger, as though he could have somehow prevented my run-in with a vicious dog.

At the uncomfortable beginning edge of Chicken Out Ridge, I wanted him to do the same for Mount Borah, to hold out his hand and drag me across the jagged edge of the knife. But he was already out of sight, somewhere amid the boulders, and my only decision was to follow. I crawled over the rocks, my pounding heart and shallow breaths only partially distracting me from the bewildering drop to either side. Rarely did my hands leave the ground, and I often ended up on my belly, clinging to each side of a rock as I slithered forward. When I reached the final saddle and discovered it was coated in snow, I began to hyperventilate. I turned my back to the trail and thought about New Jersey, about the South, about home, until my breathing calmed down and I could turn to face the narrow, icy bridge. I dug my fingers into the grainy snow and crept through Geoff's widely spaced footprints.

Finally on the other side of the knife ridge, looking toward the mellow final ascent of the peak, every fear I had been pushing back slammed me all at once. I was going to have to cross that entire thing again just to get home. I couldn't face crossing that entire thing again. But without it, I was stuck on a mountain at 12,000 feet. If I refused to cross it, someone was going to have to helicopter me home — in spite of my fear, a fate that seemed worse than death.

I felt a cold drop of liquid hit my cheek and looked up. In all of my struggle and concentration, I had failed to notice the dark clouds that had coated the hazy sky overhead. It looked like a typical afternoon storm, but I hadn't heard any thunder. Another drop of water, sharper than the first, hit the skin on my arms, and then another. They were so thick I could see them falling from the sky, slamming into the rocks and accumulating in translucent layers. It seemed a strange thing for rain to do, but as I looked closer, I could see flecks of white. A white powder coat started to cover the mountain. Powder almost as white as ... snow. It was snowing. Snowing in July.

Quickly, the storm amped up to monster-sized flakes that began to gather on my skin. They hit my exposed shoulders and soaked into my cotton tank top. They turned my legs red beneath a woefully unprotective pair of shorts. I was dressed for July's heat and it was snowing. I was hours from my tent and car and it was snowing. I was on the wrong side of the scariest ridge in the world and it was snowing. I could not breathe. I could not think. All I could do was curl up in the snow-coated gravel on the side of the trail and cry.

The mountain was too much. But even in my foggy state of mind, I knew that my breakdown had nothing to do with facing death and everything to do with facing fear. Geoff and probably a hundred other people that day had managed to make it over the ridge without a second thought, and even I had made it over once despite my inexperience and overcompensation.

The freak snowstorm was moving through quickly. Large windows of blue sky punctured the gray ceiling. Despite being underdressed, I didn't really feel all that cold. All I needed was to clear my head and start moving again and I would live through it. But that knowledge was not enough. I wasn't even sure I wanted to live through it. I knew that I never wanted to feel that kind of fear again.

Twenty minutes later, Geoff found me still sitting on the side of the trail, covered in a half inch of wet snow. Tear stains streaked my cheeks. I did not look at him. I did not know what to say. I could only be honest.

"I'm sorry," I said. "I freaked out."

"Are you OK?" Geoff asked.

"I'm fine," I said. "I just had this freak out that I needed to get through. I think I'm through it."

"Are you sure?"

"Yeah, I'm OK. Did you make it to the peak?"

"I came about 200 feet short," Geoff said. "I stopped to wait for you for a while. When I didn't see you, I walked back to look for you. I walked for a while."

"I've been stopped for a while," I said. "Plus it took me about a year to get over that ridge.

"Aren't you cold?"

"I guess."

"You're shivering."

"Yeah."

"Well," Geoff said. "It's late. We should go back."

I nodded. "Ok."

I followed him over the old snow on the saddle, standing upright as I shadowed his every step. He helped me over a ten-foot scramble and guided me across the narrow boulder field, never drifting very far from my position and always stopping to look back. On the other side of the ridge, streaks of sunlight started to break through the clouds. The dark storm was moving quickly to the south, leaving deeply clear blue sky in its place. I looked at the peak, now snow-capped and sparkling pink beneath the first hints of evening light.

"I'm sorry I kept you from getting to the peak," I said.

"It doesn't really matter," Geoff said. "I guess that just means we'll have to come back here."

I let out a forced little laugh. "Are you kidding? You'd drag me back here? I'm pretty sure that's the most I'll ever see of Mount Borah. Maybe if anyone asks, I'll just tell them I made it to the peak."

"So are you feeling better?" Geoff asked.

I held up my hands, still shaking and numb. My legs tingled beneath the continuous stabbing of what felt like a thousand invisible needles. Such was the painful price of rewarming. My palms were raw from the lava rock and the crawling, and one of my knees was for an unknown reason bleeding. My feet ached with every long downhill step. My awareness was still returning in fits and gasps as my thoughts continued to drift into the safety of memories. My mind was exhausted from my curled-up period of self-inflicted shock. I knew we still had a long way down and it would nearly be dark by the time we got there. But my heart was absolutely soaring.

"Yeah," I said. "Yeah, I do feel better."

Rohn, Alaska
February 27, 2008

The Rohn cabin was smaller and dumpier than I ever imagined.

I had been warned not to expect much. After my night on the pass, I should have been overjoyed to see it even if it were an abandoned single-wide with a tarp for a roof. But I could find little relief in the one-room log structure that was no larger than the Forest Service cabins Geoff and I would rent out for weekends in the woods. It was surrounded by wind-scoured canvas tents where the people who volunteered for the Iditarod Trail Dog Sled Race probably slept, and I guessed the little cabin was where all of those people, perhaps a half dozen or more, gathered during the day.

Snowmobile parts and firewood logs were strewn everywhere. Foot-packed trails in the snow led to an outhouse and meandered around the tents and cut a bumpy path to the air strip. Rohn was a homeless camp of the worst kind — a homeless camp in a place where it was impossible to live without a home. Although my disappointment with what should have been a relief of civilization was not justified, I could not contain it.

I parked my bike in the sun, hoping against hope that dim rays of solar light would somehow thaw its frozen parts in the subzero air. I knocked tentatively on the cabin door because I had been warned that the dog sled race volunteers were not always friendly to cyclists. Maybe they didn't like us because we weren't part of their race and therefore not their problem. Or maybe it was because our sub-culture clashed with theirs even as we muscled our way into their territory. I did-n't really know why they might not be nice to me, I only knew that after a hard night of homelessness and an early morning dip in the creek, the last thing I wanted to deal with was a grumpy human.

A gruff man with a full salt-and-pepper beard answered the door and imme-diately frowned at me. "Iditasport?" he asked.

"Uh, yeah," I said.

"Your tent's not up yet," he said.

"My tent?"

"Rob came in late last night because they couldn't get over the pass. They've spent the whole morning breaking trail, so he hasn't had time to put your tent up yet."

"Oh, OK," I said, feeling completely dejected. I half hoped the man wouldn't invite me inside the cabin, because I just wanted to ride off down the trail and never think about that place again. In retrospect, he might have been doing me a favor by simply closing the door. But instead he opened it wider and let me in.

I noticed the wood stove burning hot and asked him if I could take off my boots. He waved his hand. I pulled off the ice-coated boots and set them next to the stove, then peeled off my socks. One of them dripped cold water on the floor. When the man wasn't looking, I wrung the wet sock into the ash basin beneath the stove and hung both socks on a small rope. I set my boots aside and hoped that the unfortunately waterproof shell would somehow let the soles dry out quickly.

"Would you like some pancakes?" the man grunted.

"Pancakes?" I asked. The word seemed so foreign. Was this man who so clear-ly despised my presence actually asking if he could make me pancakes?

"I make pancakes for all you racers," he said. "That's my job. My name's Jasper. I do the cooking for everyone. Your people tend to stay here longer than the mushers, but at least you're not as messy. Those guys leave their garbage everywhere."

"Really?" I said. "You make pancakes for the cyclists and runners, too?"

"Yeah," he said. "I would have made breakfast for all those guys this morn-ing, but they all got up and left at 2 a.m. I'm a nice guy, but I'm not that nice."

I was beginning to think that his gruff man with the grizzly bear exterior may have actually been the nice, kind-hearted guy he said he was. Without even wait-ing for my confirmation, he fired up his propane stove and began mixing up pan-cake batter, even though it was after 11 a.m.

"So everyone left together this morning?" I asked.

"Mostly," he said. "They all came in last night. Rob and the others couldn't drive their snowmachines over the pass to build the trail, so all the bikers bottle-necked in the gorge, eight or nine right on top of each other. They took turns breaking trail and got here sometime last night. Boy, was that a rough night. All of them stacked on top of each other in this cabin, all of them mad about the trail, but it wasn't our fault. This is a bad year! A lot of brush, a lot of snow, a lot of open water. It's a lot of work for us to build those trails. I don't think they realize it."

"Those guys slept in here?"

"Yeah. I told you, Rob's been busy breaking trail, so he hasn't put up your tent yet."

Jasper handed me a small stack of pancakes. I chopped large triangles with a plastic fork and struggled to stuff them down. After my major bonk the night before, I assumed the food would start sliding down freely. But despite an almost complete lack of energy, I still had no appetite.

Jasper saw me eyeing the candy on the table and told me I could take some.

"Some of the bikers left it here," he said. "Like we're a garbage dump or something. It's expensive to fly trash out of here. Real expensive."

Just as I was finishing my pancakes, a dark-haired, younger man threw open the door and followed a rush of cold air into the cabin.

"You Jill?" he asked.

"Yeah. Are you Rob?"

Rob nodded. "Sorry, but I haven't set the tent up yet. But I'm working on it right now. Go ahead, have some lunch, and hopefully I'll have it ready to go in an hour or so."

Rob was the race volunteer for the Iditarod Trail Invitational. I had heard his name mentioned in the slew of information at the pre-race meeting, but had forgotten that someone specific would be waiting in Rohn for cyclists, skiers and runners to go through. I felt a tinge of shame about how long it had taken me to get there. Surely Rob had some record of when I left Puntilla. If he put two and two together, he'd know I was having trouble.

"Actually, I'm thinking about getting going pretty soon here," I said. "While it's still light out."

An understanding frown settled into Rob's face. "You spent the night out last night?" he asked. I nodded. "You should sleep here. Just for a while. This is a good place to sleep. Out there, that's not such a good place to sleep."

Fear ripped away at my sense of urgency to finish the long race. My will to continue was already fading with each starchy bite of pancakes. Now I had a voice of reason urging me not to go on until I was absolutely ready. A perfect excuse that I did not want. My disgust for Rohn was growing by the minute. And yet I wanted to stay more than anything. But I knew if I did stay, I might not regain the will to leave under my own power.

"Stay!" Jasper boomed. "You can help us out. We need someone to chop wood, sort dog food, lay straw, that kind of stuff. Stay for a week or two, till all the dog teams come through. Free room and board. Free flight out. It's the deal of a lifetime!"

That option sounded worse than finishing the race barefoot, but I didn't want to voice my opinion of Rohn out loud to Jasper, the self-proclaimed "mayor" of

Rohn according to a sign posted outside the cabin door. So I just smiled and said, "Doesn't sound half bad."

"Not bad at all," Jasper said. "We'll even give you your own tent."

"Sleep," Rob said. "You'll feel so much better if you do."

"You can sleep in here," Jasper said, "while Rob gets the tent set up. I'll clear some stuff off here," he pointed to a wood bunk bed just a few feet from the kitchen and moved to clear a sleeping bag and clothing off the bottom platform. "Here, I'll make you a bed."

I nodded gratefully at the gruff dog sled race volunteer, who owed me nothing but still offered me everything he had. It wasn't much, but out in the Alaska Bush in the prison of winter, it was the difference between living and dying. Even if I was not overjoyed with it, I was truly grateful for it, and was even more grateful for the Alaska Bush code of share and share equally.

Rob rushed outside, and Jasper and I were alone again. "I know this is a terrible thing to ask, and you can say no," I started.

"And?" he said somewhat loudly. I took a deep breath. He had been generous to me and I was already trying his patience.

"Well, my bike is frozen. I dropped it in the river. By accident. But it's all coated in ice, all the moving parts, and ..."

"And you want to bring it inside to thaw it out?"

"Yeah," I said.

"Well, go out and get it," he said. "It can stay in here for a while until the others get back. Then there'll be no room for it. But it should be enough time to dry out a bit."

"Thank you!" I exclaimed. "Thank you!" I darted out the door in my down booties to grab the bike and wheel it in. I unrolled my frost-coated sleeping bag and hung it next to all my other crap, crowding out nearly all of the extra space next to the stove. I spread out my sleeping pad on the empty bottom bunk and laid on top of it in my long underwear, shivering quietly beneath a flood of apprehension and self doubt, pretending to sleep.

I even caught a few restless snoozes before Ted Calahane walked in, several hours after I had arrived. Ted and Jasper talked quietly for several minutes about the other racers, the wind, something about a hard night on the pass.

"That Jill?" Ted said.

"The woman? Yeah, that's her," Jasper said. It hadn't occurred to me before in this race that I could be seen as "the woman." Maybe that's what netted me this special treatment in Rohn. Either way, I wasn't complaining.

Ted sat next to me on the bottom bunk, not even acknowledging that I might have actually been sleeping. I pretended to stir from a deep sleep and blinked at him.

"Hi Ted, how are you feeling?" I asked.

"Look at my nose?" he asked me. I sat up. His nose was mildly pink and flaking a little skin. It looked like a minor sunburn. "Does it look really bad?"

"It's a little red," I said.

"I think I frostbit it last night," Ted said. "I had to bivy right up on top of Rainy Pass. It was awful. All that wind. Hit me right in the face. I didn't really know if I'd make it through the night."

"I had to sleep out too," I said. "I was about ten miles down from the pass. It wasn't that bad where I was." Of course I didn't mention my own hyperventilating certainty of doom and falling in the stream in the morning. No need to spread that around.

"But you're OK?" I asked.

"I guess," he said.

"How did you get across the steam?" I asked.

"The stream?"

"The open water."

"Oh," he said. "I followed the footprints around to that narrow crossing. Then I picked up my bike," he said, lifting his arms like he was holding something heavy. "And then threw it over the bank. Just tossed it. Then I stepped back, took a running start, and jumped over myself."

"You threw your bike over the gap?" I asked. "Weren't you worried that it wouldn't make it or slide back into the stream?"

"Honestly, at that point, I didn't care," he said. "How'd you get through?"

"I just walked through the water with garbage bags on my feet," I said. "I dropped my bike in the creek by accident. It was actually kind of an ordeal."

"Did all of your stuff get wet?"

"I caught it before it did," I said.

"Yeah, I didn't care if my stuff got wet," he said. "I knew I was going to carry it back here either way. I'm done with this race. This is enough. I came here to have fun. This isn't fun."

"You're quitting?"

"I'm definitely quitting."

"You should sleep on it," I said, echoing Rob's soothing tones.

"I don't need to sleep on it. I don't need to think about it any more. I'm quitting here. I don't care how much it costs. What about you? Do you want to split a flight out?"

"I'm going on," I said.

"Are you sure?"

I let that question simmer in silence, and Ted knew exactly what I meant.

"Let me know," he said. And with that, he stood up and started stripping off his wet clothing.

I tossed and turned with my uncomfortable thoughts until late afternoon, when Rob walked back in and announced he had the tent up. I stood up and started gathering up gear.

"Are you leaving now?" he asked.

"Actually, I haven't been able to sleep at all, so I think I'm going to go into the tent and see if it works better for me there."

"OK," he said slowly. His wavering voice told me he was worried about me.

I walked outside just as Bill and Kathi Merchant, the couple who organized the race and who were attempting to ride all the way to Nome, rolled up on their bikes. I had expected them to catch me but hoped against hope that it wouldn't be in the purgatory of Rohn. Both had participated in the race since the early part of the decade, and both had completed the race to McGrath several times. I looked up to them like heroes, for everything they had done and everything they were trying to accomplish. They accepted my desire to take up the Iditarod challenge and encouraged me early in my training, even when many others told me I was in way over my head. I didn't want them to join me in my weakest and most broken moments.

"Jill!" Bill yelled jovially. "Fancy seeing you here! I thought you were long gone by now!"

"I'm having a tough time," I admitted.

"You're doing great!" Bill said. "Making great time! No need to hurry."

He turned to chat with Jasper and another Iditarod volunteer who had just driven up on a snowmobile. I suddenly realized Bill may have all the answers I needed. I waited several seconds and then impatiently gestured to regain his attention. He stopped talking to the volunteers and turned back to me.

"Do you know where Geoff is?" I asked.

"Geoff? He's great. He's so much fun. I love him to death. We had a great time up at Finger Lake."

"You saw him at Finger Lake?" I said. "How is he doing?"

"Oh, I'm sorry, Geoff had to scratch," Bill said. "Yeah, he really hurt his ankle. Did something to tweak it. He could run on it, but he couldn't walk. And he felt so bad when he had to walk back to Finger Lake after leaving for Puntilla. I felt kinda bad, too. It was kinda my fault. I heralded him with trail stories and got him all fired up and sent him back out even after he knew he wanted to quit."

"Geoff quit?" I said weakly. "Geoff's out?"

"Yeah. He already flew out of Finger Lake," Bill said. "Probably back in Anchorage right now. It's too bad. Hope he can come back next year."

I just turned away and mumbled a quick thanks, saying something about being underdressed for the cold before I hustled into the unheated tent. I spread out my sleeping back on the straw-covered snow and crawled inside. I shivered with fear and devastation as the most uncomfortable anxieties I had experienced in the race coursed through my veins. Geoff was gone. Geoff wasn't coming. Geoff was out of the race. Geoff was flying back home. I couldn't think of worse news to hear at that moment. Bill could have told me the weather forecast called for the blizzard of the century, that it was going to be 80 below before wind chill, and, oh yeah, there's a pack of rabid wolves on the prowl over the Farewell Burn. Any of those situations would have sounded more comforting than the news that Geoff had dropped out. This outpost of civilization was all I had left and I was alone, so alone, so completely and vastly alone.

Such a complete state of loneliness was more than I could bear with what I had left of my strung-out emotions, but the thought of quitting didn't rest easy, either. I couldn't quit because I was lonely. I couldn't quit because I was scared. I had expected all these things, plus 80-below temperatures and rabid wolves, so I couldn't let myself down now.

There wasn't a thing I could think about doing that didn't make me feel physically ill. The sickness was so debilitating that I felt I couldn't do anything but linger in limbo, not moving but not sleeping, not doing anything constructive but stewing in a reel of unhealthy downtime, burning up hours I did not have. Everything I did only made me feel worse.

Rob came in and asked me if I wanted dinner. I told him I did not. The hours slunk by. I drifted in and out of sleep, never for more than 20 or 30 minutes at a time as Rob shuffled in and out of the tent, lighting a propane heater and opening cans of soup on a camp stove. Ted eventually came in and went to sleep. I thought about the Farewell Burn, the frozen wasteland. I thought about the way so many of nature's cruelest elements condensed in a single spot, a place where my weak and broken body could be ripped apart, strewn asunder, and swallowed by ice and snow, never to be found.

This was no longer about cycling and no longer about the race. My voice of doubt had been right — this was my life. Only now it was my life without Geoff, my life without hope, my life without real reason to go on. Going back out into the cold and unknown seemed like calculated suicide, but suicide could not possibly be any worse than the limbo and loneliness. I closed my eyes and fell back asleep for a final time.

.

Salt Lake City, Utah
June 2002

"You off to go training again?" my roommate, Curt, asked as I polished off an afternoon bowl of Alphabits and strapped on my bike helmet.

"Practicing," I said. "When you don't know what you're doing, it's called practicing."

I wheeled Geoff's old rigid mountain bike through the living room. The chain clicked and the brakes squealed. The noises were becoming harder to ignore. I had long since given up looking for the source of another, increasingly louder rattling. There was creaking, too, but diagnostics were impossible when those sounds seemed to emanate from every part of the bike.

But the bike did have two wheels and did move forward. So, I reasoned, it was everything I needed. Geoff offered to let me borrow it while he was away for the summer. He told me if I wanted to actually complete a long bicycle tour, I was going to have to learn to ride a bicycle first.

"You're going to have to teach me how to do that thing with the thumbs," I had told him as we drove home from a camping trip two months earlier. We had been crossing the desert for the better part of four hours and had big visions of open roads in our heads.

"What, shifting?" Geoff had replied incredulously.

"Yeah, shifting," I said. I was 22 years old and I had not pedaled a bicycle more than 30 miles in my adult life. The last bike I had owned was a Huffy ten-speed that I received for my 10th birthday. It sat in my parents' garage collecting dust from the day I received my driver's license forward.

But in the way most hobbies take hold, cycling came to me in a flash of inspiration during that long drive home from yet another backpacking weekend in Moab. I gazed out the window at the snow-crusted hills, which were still struggling to emerge from winter in mid-April, and asked Geoff if he had ever done any touring by bicycle.

"Just a little. Why?" he had asked. "Are you interested in bike touring?"

I told him that maybe I was, that maybe cycling seemed like a great way to travel from one point to another. That it might even been a great way to get from once side of the country to the other. We launched into a long discussion about possibilities and logistics of bicycle travel when Geoff asked me if I even knew how to ride a bicycle.

"Probably," I told him. "That's one of those things we don't forget, right?" That admission sparked a new conversation about the logistics and possibilities of simply riding a bicycle. Geoff concluded that if we were going to achieve my stream-of-consciousness-sparked dream of riding a bicycle across the country, I was going to have to "practice" riding a bicycle. So that's what I vowed to do during the months that Geoff was away on a rafting trip down the Green River, chasing his own expedition dreams.

"So are you still falling over on a regular basis?" Curt asked me as I lifted up the rear wheel of Geoff's bike and vigorously spun the crank, half-heartedly trying to locate the source of the new squeaking.

"Not on the street anymore," I said. "And it was just that one time. I forgot to put my foot down. Oh, yeah, I guess there was the time I took a corner too sharp. Yeah, I laid the bike down then, too."

"You told me you slammed your shoulder on a tree the last time you went out," he said.

"That happened on a trail," I said. "I've started riding through Red Butte Gardens. I figured I'm on a mountain bike. I should probably try some off-road riding, get a feel for the dirt."

"Think you should learn on-road riding first," Curt said.

"Yeah, I really am getting better at that," I said. "My butt doesn't even hurt all the time any more. Mostly just after the first hour or so."

"So, are you going up to Red Butte today?"

"Probably," I said. "I'm going to do the climb up Emigration Canyon first. Geoff says training to climb is the only way I'm ever going to get over the Rocky Mountains."

"Oh, so you are training," Curt said.

"Training ... practicing ... whatever," I said. In my opinion, training was for people with hard bodies and minds solely focused on competition. Athletes trained. Novices dawdled around and increased their chances of not killing themselves. But in the end, it was all about self improvement.

"Well, I'd say you're training," Curt said. "That's what it's called when the things you do become necessary."

"I thought that was called working," I said.

"Training, working ... it's the same thing," Curt said. He laughed. "Especially when you do it every day, even if it means tipping over in the dirt."

"Well, I have to say, even tipping in the dirt beats working," I said. "Some lady called me at the Transcript today, just screaming about a mistake in her mother's obituary. I mean she was screaming at me, and crying, too. And calling me every name possible. For like a solid hour. Man, I'd rather ride a hundred miles a day than listen to that. It was like we misspelled someone's name in purpose. Like everyone at the newspaper just sits around all day staring at our computers and thinking about all the ways we can ruin people's lives."

"You mean that's not what you do?"

"Ha ha," I said. "But I'm starting to think Geoff was right. I should have given up the job and gone with them on their long river trip. Too bad I hate river trips."

"Still afraid of rafting?"

"I'm never going on another river trip again, at least not if there's rapids involved," I said.

I shook my head with rare certainty. Earlier that spring, Geoff coaxed me away from my Rapid Number Five trauma by promising me that another section of the Colorado River, Westwater Canyon, was much more gentle and easier to navigate. So in May, I reluctantly crawled into his red raft for a second time, joining Geoff and his two friends, Erin and Aaron, and their 6-month-old pit bull puppy for a quick overnight trip down the river.

I hadn't even gotten wet from splashing before Geoff steered us into the pit of a rapid called Skull and flipped the raft over in one of the first waves in the train, long before we even reached the notorious "Skull Hole" followed by the "Room of Doom" and "Rock of Shock." I had to take on those monsters myself, a helpless rag doll in the bowels of a raging cauldron, flailing my arms and gasping for air. Roiling waves grabbed me and pulled me under the river repeatedly, and the entire time, the pit bull paddled beside me and wailed.

The puppy's mournful cries continued to haunt my dreams long after Chris pulled my limp body out of the water for a second time and rowed us to dry land. So when Geoff announced he and two friends were going to spend four weeks rowing the length of the Green River during the summer, and asked me if I wanted to come, I said with absolute conviction, "No Way."

Instead, Geoff and I spent the remainder of the spring talking about bike touring, about a more distant future that involved pedaling a bicycle across the width of an entire continent. Ever since we returned from our cross-country road trip, I had an ever-more nagging suspicion that I had been presented with a crossroads in my life during the previous summer. But instead of taking one tangent or another, I had skirted every single option and gone back the way I came.

That my life actually was radically different than it had been before I traveled across the United States made this suspicion even more confusing. My landlords kicked me out of my college apartment while Geoff and I were traveling. I was homeless when we returned, so I moved into the commune-like house that Geoff occupied — a cheap-rent lifestyle shared with eight other post-college drifters. I took another newspaper job in a small rural community 35 miles west of Salt Lake City. Although that position was much more stable than my previous journalism job, driving a long backwards commute from my downtown house every day had started to wear down on my enthusiasm for working in newspapers. Geoff and I became weekend warriors, traveling south to hike and camp with a rotating group of roommates and friends. But after he left for the summer, my lifestyle quietly slipped into the driving-sitting-eating endless loop of a working drone's existence.

My co-workers always seemed to move through their days in a daze, and I found myself inclined to join them. After 45 minutes of driving alone along the hot, barren shoreline of the Salt Lake in my non-air-conditioned car, I would sit at my office desk, drenched in sweat, and think about how fake the cool air drifting down from the vents really felt. Sometimes I hated the walls of my office for holding out the sunshine and morning breezes and desert heat, but yet I couldn't imagine life without them.

I was a community news editor and news clerk. It was my job to write the fluffy feature stories for my small-town newspaper, and take calls from people whose lives seemed to revolve around weddings, anniversaries and funerals. Soon enough, I felt like my life revolved around their weddings, anniversaries and funerals. And really, when I thought about it, everyone's lives, when observed from the records we leave to future, must seem like little more than a progression of weddings, anniversaries and funerals.

The dull emptiness surrounding my latest career advancement eroded away at my rediscovered sense of duty and wore air holes into my aging wanderlust. When Geoff and I started talking about bicycle touring, I jumped on the idea with every ounce of enthusiasm and energy I could muster with my marshmallow muscles.

Between the stagnant summer days full of obituary complaints, and the long lonely evenings I spent trying to maintain my sense of individuality and space among too many roommates, I was beginning the believe cycling was my only escape. If training was something people do because it's necessary, then the future bicycle tour was my necessary journey.

I wheeled Geoff's bike out the front door and began to pedal through the visible waves of heat wafting off the pavement. I gripped my brakes at the corner stop sign and paused a few seconds before turning left onto a gradually inclined road toward the foothills. I was still tentative on the corners, slow on the climbs, and riding a borrowed bike that barely held itself together. But "training" had turned me into something new amid the discontent of my poison summer — a cyclist.

And even when the cycling became a simple extension of my routine, even when I left the house every afternoon only to ride the same hills and trails, there was something in the movement, an antidote, that felt both refreshing and regenerative. And suddenly, the 45-minute drive to and from work didn't hurt so much; the wedding announcement-frantic customers didn't scream so loud; the hot summer afternoons didn't wear so deep and the evenings didn't feel so lonely, even as I spent more and more time alone in the sun.

Cycling offered a new balance that showed me there was still the possibility I could be happy in my drive-sit-eat lifestyle, because always in the back of my mind I remembered the roads still stretched out limitlessly, and the simple act of turning cranks still had the potential to jolt my weary heart to new highs.

After I had a few miles under my legs, my mind always returned to the planned bike tour. I thought often about the simple rewards in just loading a bike with everything I need in the world and setting out toward the great unknown. I rode past the university and turned to pedal up Emigration Canyon, a gently winding road that led to the place whereseveral of my teenage boyfriends used to take me to nervously hold hands and hope it led to something more. The sweaty haze of hard pedaling had a way of dredging up powerful nostalgia, and I often found myself thinking back to scenes with more clarity than I had even known when they were fresh and new.

The top of Emigration Canyon was also a favorite of Spencer, the boy who never loved me, but who always had a way of making the 16-year-old version of myself feel ecstatic and free just the same. He would always point out to the black void beyond the glittering city lights and tell me stories about the West Desert. He would tell me about its beauty and its magic, and I believed him, unconditionally. That was back when the whole world was still a great unknown.

But then I became an adult. I got a career-type job. I learned to ride a bicycle. I had been up Emigration Canyon dozens of times, by myself, and I no longer wondered about the strange landscapes that stretched beyond the horizon, beyond the West Desert. I was 22 years old, and I had seen what lay beyond the West Desert. I was 22 years old, and I worked out there. I spent every day half sleepwalking among its storefronts and suburban tract housing. I knew now that its magic was simply another realm for weddings, anniversaries and funerals.

Despite my well-earned cynicism, the cyclist in me still stopped at the old Emigration Canyon overlook, every time. The cyclist in me was still amazed by the power of the space, by the idea that below me there were a half million people going about their workaday lives, and I was alone on a mountain, far above the city grid, far away from all the shimmering glass and concrete, with nothing but me and my — well, Geoff's — bike. But maybe, just maybe, that was all I needed.

I felt more tired than usual as I descended the canyon, death-gripping the brake levers with all the fear of gravity that still coursed through my novice veins. But I was becoming a more assured cyclist with every ride, even as the daily workouts started to wear my muscles down. I felt fatigued and sore, but competent, just like a real athlete. I smiled at the thought of myself as an athlete, the kind of person who could call herself a cyclist. The kind of person who "trained."

I veered onto a Red Butte Gardens trail and hit the brakes hard as the bike bounced over the bumps in the dirt. The rear wheel began to fishtail and I lurched forward, hurtling over the handlebars and landing in a crumpled heap amid scrub oak and stinging nettle. The transition from coasting smooth pavement to crashing face first into the dirt came so quickly that all I could do as the dust settled was lay there, stunned, wondering if I had been hit by a car.

When I remembered that I had purposely veered onto a dirt trail and instantly lost control of the bike, I stood up, brushed myself off, and looked around for blood stains or other signs of damage.

When the body scan came up clean, I picked up Geoff's bike to commence the damage assessment. I noticed the rear tire was flat. The rear brake arm had also snapped loose and I did not know how to fix it. I let out a long, defeated sigh, picked up the rickety old bike, and began the three-mile walk home.

My legs were noticeably stiff and my hip felt bruised and sore as I limped down the sidewalk. The new Red Butte Gardens debacle made solid crash number three on Geoff's bike, and that wasn't even counting the time I forgot to put my feet down at a stoplight. Three crashes, maybe five if I counted the soft falls, did not seem like a wonderful record for a few weeks of practicing the art of riding a bike. I had crashed a mere two times in a whitewater raft and swore off river rafting forever, and yet there was something about the bike that kept coaxing me back despite the continuing violence.

I laughed about how pathetic I must have looked limping down the street, pushing a rusty, half-broken bicycle beside me. And yet I knew when I returned to my commune of a house, I was going to admit to Curt that I had crashed again; I was going to ask him how to repair the brake and wheel, and I was going to go right back out there the following day.

Bison Camp, Alaska
February 28, 2008

A dim propane light flickered against the shadows in a world dominated by darkness.

My nose and one eye were pressed against a small opening in my sleeping bag. I could see frost clinging to an inside wall of the canvas tent.

I looked at my watch. It was 3 a.m. Thursday. I did the time conversion in my head. 16 hours. I had been in Rohn for 16 hours. I wondered how many hours had been productively used sleeping and eating, and how many had been utterly wasted in stress-streaked limbo. I sat up from the straw-covered snow and blinked to clear my vision. Rob was still awake, sitting silently on a bucket near the camp stove and staring off into space.

"How are you feeling?" he asked groggily.

"Good," I said. "I feel good. Much, much better."

"That's good," he said. He reached over to stir several cans of soup that were boiling on the stove as I kicked out of my sleeping bag.

"You going to the bathroom?" he asked.

"No," I said. "I think I'm going to get going. I've certainly been here long enough."

"You're leaving?" he asked. He sounded surprised. After all this time, he must have assumed I had settled in for the long haul, waiting for the flight to freedom with Ted. The idea that I would stay in Rohn for 16 hours and then just get up and leave under my own volition seemed a foreign concept to him. Either racers race, or they quit. But Rob didn't argue. "You want some soup before you go?"

I shook my head.

"You have everything you need?"

"I have my drop bag outside," I said. "It has more food than I could ever eat." How extremely true this statement was, Rob would never understand.

"Well, good luck," Rob said. "You'll like it out there. This is a good race. I did it once several years ago, on foot. A lot of people asked me why I did it on foot, but for me, it was the easiest way to go. You bikers, you can move when you're riding, but most of the time, I just feel bad for you dragging those anchors."

"Did you finish the race?" I asked.

"Oh yeah," Rob said. "I finished. Only once. I've come back here every year as a volunteer. I would never race it again, but I do love this race. When you finish, you'll understand."

"Do you think I still have a shot at finishing?" I asked.

"If you leave here, you'll finish," Rob said.

I walked into the demon cold, which, after four days, seem to have had a little of the edge worn off its ungodliness. It no longer cut so deep. I wheeled my bike to the point where the Rohn spur trail met the main trail. Then I strapped on my gear, checked the tire pressure, tested my freewheel, oiled my chain. I was stalling. I was undoubtedly stalling.

Rob's little canvas tent glowed timid orange against the unending blackness. If there was anything I was certain of, it was that I was completely uncertain about moving on. Rob may have finished this race once, but he did not understand what it was like to be a woman, a scared little Mormon girl from Salt Lake City, out there in the big bad Alaska Bush. My only lifeline, Geoff, was out of the race and likely out of the region. It was only bound to get worse for me down the trail, and finishing was anything but a given.

But there was one other certainty in my mind — the certainty that I could no longer bear the uncertainty. I could no longer linger in limbo. The longer I stalled, the further I sank into dull madness. I was going to have to decide right there whether I was going to push for McGrath or get on a plane back to Anchorage with Ted and never look back. Either way, I would have to accept the consequences. There was no going back to the start, not any more. I knew there was a reason I had planned so diligently for the race, trained all winter for the race, spent all of my free time thinking about the race.

"If only I could remember what that reason was," I thought as I mounted my bicycle and pedaled into the dark. And with that, I was finally moving down the trail.

The decision to keep going — even if it had been made in a fleeting moment of frustration — did help me feel better as I pedaled onto the Kuskokwim River. The smooth surface of the river was windswept of snow and sparkling with glare ice. The smooth wheels of my bike wobbled and washed sideways. The Iditarod had become a slick, treacherous trail that had to be negotiated under the constant threat of body slam.

Still, I hadn't been able ride my bike for more than 100 yards at a time since before I reached Puntilla Lake two days and 45 miles before. The act of pedaling felt amazing, and I wanted to keep it up.

I pedaled tentatively over the slippery surface, every once in a while jumping off the saddle when the rear tire washed out. I bounced over driftwood and increased my speed on the gravel shoreline. For the first time in the entire race, I felt like I was really mountain biking. And mountain biking was fun! I smiled as I wove around the myriad obstacles, conquering them with glee before stopping to shine my light around the icy river bed, searching for the next trail marker.

Eventually, the markers led into the woods. After I left the river, the snow-covered trail took me on a rollercoaster ride over steep, narrow hills and snowmobile moguls. The terrain became increasingly more difficult to navigate and my loaded, fat-tire bike became much harder to control. I started spilling over into the snow. At one point, I lost control of the bike, planted my front wheel in a snow bank and went flying over the handlebars. I landed mere inches from a spruce tree. It was small but solid, with definite bone-breaking potential.

I realized that out there, where the closest hospital was in Anchorage and I was thousands of miles away from anywhere else, was not the place to break a bone. As much as a renewed focus on the technical terrain was replacing my more abstract fears, the Iditarod Trail was not the place to push my limited skills in snow-bike free-riding. If I didn't have the skills to ride the trail flawlessly, then I had to conserve. I shuddered at the realization, because I knew it meant more walking.

I alternated walking and riding until it was nearly dawn, when I saw a small headlamp bobbing on the hillside in the near distance. Its presence confused me. Besides Ted, Bill and Kathi, I didn't think there was another rider in front or behind me for dozens of miles, and I was certain that none of the cyclists behind me had left Rohn before I did.

After a few minutes, I realized the rider was approaching me. As he pulled up next to me, I realized he was the Euro cyclist I had eaten breakfast with at Shell Lake. Where had he come from? It was possible he had moved through Rohn while I was sleeping. After all, I spent more than 10 hours huddled in that tent, lost in fitful daydreams and oblivious to the world around me. He probably just slipped quietly in and out of the depressing compound like the stoic European that he was. But why was he pedaling backward on the trail?

He stopped and shook his head.

"Why are you going backward on the trail?" I asked.

He shrugged. I repeated myself, louder, in that stupid arrogant way in which Americans assume that if English is not understood the first time, it will somehow make more sense at higher volume.

"Impossible," he replied. "Impossible."

"What's impossible?" I asked. "The trail? Is there sometime wrong with the trail up ahead?"

He shrugged again. "Impossible."

He followed me to a point where the trail stopped at the base of a frozen waterfall. The steep pitch was coated in rolling sheets of wet ice, like a stop-motion sculpture of whitewater cascading off hidden rocks. I looked around for the next trail marker. It was nowhere to be seen. It was like the trail just dead ended at the river, as though the frozen waterfall was the destination we had pedaled 220 miles to see. I squinted into the creeping, cloudy dawn, looking for any sign of continuation. As I scanned the horizon, my headlamp caught the reflection of a trial marker, planted at least 50 vertical feet above our heads at the top of the waterfall.

"We have to go up there?" I said, loudly, hoping the Euro cyclist would somehow understand.

"Impossible," he repeated. The only word he knew. I turned to him and gave him my most earnest look, speaking as forcefully as I could muster. "Well, we have to try," I said. He raised his eyebrows. It sounded stupid to me too, but we had already come so far. "We have to try," I repeated.

I stretched my ice cleats around my boots and began to kick up one side of the waterfall, where the ice was steeper but presented more hand holds in the rock walls that lined the edge. As I walked, the bike's tires washed out and the bike tipped over. I didn't think I would be able to keep it upright, so I left it on its side where the pedals could dig in and give me another point of traction.

My ice cleats, mostly untested before the race, were too big for my feet, and they kept slipping off my boots on the wet ice. Every time one came off, the Euro cyclist yelled, "Hello!" I quickly learned this meant I needed to turn around and collect my lost cleat.

After the third 'Hello,' I looked back and realized I had to backtrack several yards. I leveraged my bike like an ice ax, squatting and inching downward until I could retrieve the cleat. A stood up and carefully lifted one boot to pull it back on, my other foot washed out. I hit the ice in a full-on body slam, right hip first, clutching my bike as we spun together all the way down to the bottom of the frozen waterfall. I let out a roar of frustration and clutched my bruised hip. Injury seemed likely, but even worse was the thought of going back to Rohn. The pain of the fall was nothing compared to the prospect of never getting past that insignificant section of trail.

"OK?" the Euro cyclist said weakly.

"Impossible," I replied.

I strapped on my cleats and tried once more. My hip throbbed painfully and I fretted about the possibility I had pulled a muscle or worse. I needed that hip to ride my bike. Even worse, I needed that hip just to walk my bike. Walking had been as of yet my most useful ability.

The cleats miraculously stayed on my feet as I slowly kicked another path up the wet ice. I let out a cheer when I achieved the top, gratefully wheeling my bicycle onto soft, sticky snow.

Unfortunately, the Euro cyclist was still hundreds of feet away, much too far to throw back my cleats. But without them, he had no way of kicking up the ice in my path. I wandered around the top of the falls, looking for a way around the ice, but the surrounding cliffs were too steep. They would be difficult to scramble up or down, even without a bike.

"You'll have to walk up!" I yelled down to the cyclist. He shook his head.

"Turn over your bike and push it in front of you!" I yelled. I knew it was a terrible idea. The thin sheet of water on top of the ice was too slippery for a single pedal to provide enough grip for the weight of a bike and a person, and that method was just asking for a similar injury to the one I had just sustained.

But the Euro cyclist didn't understand me anyway. He turned around and disappeared behind one of the cliffs, which I assumed meant he would continue looking for his own way around. There was nothing I could do to help him, so, guiltily, I limped away from the waterfall and straddled by bike once more.

After about 45 minutes of pedaling into the brightening morning, the Euro cyclist passed me again.

"You made it!" I exclaimed. He smiled and held his arm out, pointing straight up and curling his other arm as though he was trying to indicate that he had actually climbed one of the cliffs somehow, while hoisting his bike.

I held my thumbs up. "You're a superstar," I said, and he grinned.

I amped up my pace and we rode together for a while. The trail flattened out and continued to be mostly well-packed and ridable, enjoyably so as we floated atop shallow powder over Farewell Lake through a web of weaving bicycle tracks. The sun felt warmer than it had during the entire trip. I stripped down to my minimum layers and still sweated. If I had not known better, I would have guessed the temperature was 50 degrees above zero, although the ice building up inside my insulated water bottle proved the air was still well below freezing. The pain in my hip hovered near screaming level when I walked, but did not feel too bad as I turned pedals. I really, really hoped the pedal turning would continue and the walking would cease.

But the further we pedaled from the river, the hillier the terrain became. The trail did indeed stay hard packed, but it rolled over a sequence of short hills so steep that I had to kick steps into the snow to keep from sliding down as I walked up. The Euro cyclist eventually left me behind as I struggled with the steps. Every time I hopped off the bike to walk, my hip throbbed and burned. I imagined a torn muscle or severed tendon, but it was likely just a deep bruise. My hip injury didn't seem to get any worse as the day wore on. It just protested every step with searing hatred.

It was all I could do to stop at the bottom of a hill, take a few deep breaths, clench my teeth, take a few steps up the hill, scream out in pain, take a few more breaths, scream again, take a few more steps, etc. My pace again slowed to a crawl. I rifled through my backpack for my aspirin. When I couldn't find the drugs in there, I tore open each of my bike bags, hoping it had somehow ended up in the wrong spot.

No such luck. My medicine bag was gone, likely abandoned in the tent in Rohn, and I was miles beyond Farewell Lake with no aspirin, no caffeine, no menthol patches, no glucosamine. All I had left was my sweat-soaked extra clothing that had frozen into tight balls, food that I could not eat, and a sleeping bag I hoped I'd never use again. As long as I was walking anyway, I might as well just lose the bike. I didn't want any of it.

It was 4 p.m. when I reached Bison Camp, 45 miles in 12 hours. Not terrible by general Iditarod standards, but probably pretty terrible by 2008 standards when I considered how much of that last section of trail was ridable. The strongmen probably blasted through in five or six hours. Still, at least I didn't feel exhausted anymore. I actually had something similar to an appetite.

I walked inside the large canvas tent, where the Euro cyclist had already built a raging fire in the wood stove. I gathered up buckets of snow to make water and set my aluminum package of tuna directly on the stovetop to thaw. We ate together in silence and he offered me a hunk of cheese.

"It's Italian," he purred, and I smiled. The Euro cyclist was Italian. I offered up my package of mostly crushed wheat thins, and he scooped them up gleefully. I couldn't help but laugh out loud at the situation ... a white-bread-raised Utahn and an Italian, sharing our meager but eclectic trail meals out here in this frozen wasteland, this Buffalo Camp, on the edge of Alaska's Farewell Burn.

I dug through my backpack again, only to realize my headlamp was missing. I had it when I left Rohn in the morning, so it must have fallen off my head sometime after dawn, maybe during one of my many crashes. I swore out loud but knew I couldn't let the careless loss discourage me. There was nothing I could do to bring it back.

I marched outside with my pocket knife and began sawing at my backup light, which I had taped to my bike's front rack like a headlight, and grabbed a spare strap. Back inside the tent, I went to work with my duct tape, fashioning a new headlamp that I could attach to my head with the metal clasp on the four-foot strap. All that time, the Italian watched me and munched his Italian cheese as though nothing I was doing seemed strange or out of place. How quickly we become citizens of the Iditarod Trail.

The Italian was settling down to sleep on the straw just as Bill and Kathi caught up to us. Bill was glancing at a thermometer on a post when I walked outside to meet him.

"Wow," he said. "What a balmy day this has been!" I looked over at the thermometer. It was 8 degrees. Kathi began gathering snow for her own water. I sheepishly asked Bill if he had seem my headlamp.

He rifled around in his coat pocket. "You mean this?" he asked as he pulled it out. I grinned and held my mittens out to receive this most unexpected prize.

"It must have fallen off my head when I took a crash this morning," I said, trying to speak in an apologetic tone to emphasize how stupid I felt about it.

"Oh, don't worry about it," Bill said. "Happens to all of us. Why, just this morning, I was riding those trails pretty crazy, having a grand old time, flying over the handlebars and making a few of my own snow angels on the trail. And then I noticed my GPS was missing. I had it mounted on my handlebars, and now it's gone. I think it's back there in one of my snow angels."

"Oh, that's awful," I said, thinking about my own GPS, which I had spent several hundred dollars on and used continuously during the race.

"I don't need it," he said. "It was nice to have; not a necessity. Now these," he said, holding up a pair of well-worn mittens. "Now if I lost these, then I'd have problems."

I looked at my own mittens and thought about how much they meant to me. In fact, all of my meager gear ... the tattered clothing that kept me warm, the bike that moved me forward, the sleeping bag that saved my life, even the food that provided me with fuel whenever I could stuff it down ... all if it really did mean everything to me. Out on the Iditarod Trail, it was all I had, down to my $20 mittens, and it was all priceless. I smiled at this realization. How quickly we become citizens of the Iditarod Trail.

And as I talked and laughed with Bill and Kathi, I started to feel more like a real person than I had in days. They offered me their trail snacks and I began putting down food like I hadn't eaten in days, which in a way, I hadn't. Nuts, crackers, fruit leather, chocolate ... it was finally disappearing from the heavy laden bag I had hauled it in for four days. Bill and Kathi heralded me with a menagerie of trail stories from years previous. They confided in me that they were thinking of blowing through Nikolai, the next checkpoint, that night and pushing right on for McGrath.

"You guys are going to go all the way to McGrath tonight?" I asked in disbelief. The prospect of being done with the race before sleeping again ... of being done that night ... was unfathomable. And so appealing.

Stuffed full of food and feeling less pain in my hip after discovering a couple of ibuprofen in a dirty container on the tent's shelf, I could think of nothing more exciting than getting back on my bike and riding again. It was still early in a way — 6 p.m. — and Nikolai was 45 miles away, a jaunt if the trail was good, and still only about 12 hours if it wasn't. I felt like I had the energy to stay awake for days, riding a high that coursed through my veins like caffeine even when I had none.

I wheeled my bike up the last hill and looked across the Farewell Burn just as the sun set on the southern horizon. The sky bled orange as I stared in wonder at the wide river valley in front of me, coated in row after row of nearly identically sized baby spruce trees that were just starting to grow up after the place burned to nothing several years before. And right down the center of the valley, a narrow trail carved a straight white line, so flat I could trace it all the way to the horizon. It was the most beautiful landscape I had ever seen.

Telluride, Colorado
September 18, 2002

Late in the evening, it started to snow.

A little snow had never seemed that bad on a camping trip before, but then again, I had never been on a camping trip with only the limited gear I could carry on a bicycle. My comfort depended on a small backpacking tent, a rated-to-35-degrees synthetic sleeping bag, a thin jacket and a handful of cycling clothes. It seemed woefully inadequate for the circumstances, like shielding oneself with a piece of newspaper during a downpour.

"Great," I said to Geoff. "We waited out one day of rain and now it's snowing."

A mottled blanket of white had already settled over the road as swirling flakes flickered like static beneath street lights.

The mountain town of Telluride, Colo., was silent as Geoff and I walked back to our camp from the movie theater after an evening out on the town. We were five days into a planned two-week bicycle tour of southeastern Utah and southwestern Colorado, 600 miles of mountains and deserts during early fall in 2002. We had pedaled more than 150 miles since leaving Moab, Utah, earlier that week. It already seemed like a lifetime ago.

"We'll be fine," Geoff said. "Your bag seems pretty warm, doesn't it?"

"Maybe," I said. "I purposely just packed the smallest one I could find. Warmth didn't cross my mind when it was 90 degrees out a week ago."

"Well, we're at 8,000 feet now," Geoff said. "Sometimes it snows in September here."

"Clearly," I said. "At least that campground has a bathroom. If I wake up in the night all cold and wet, I'm going to sleep in there."

"Maybe we should put our food, the eggs and stuff, in there tonight," Geoff said. "In case it freezes."

"I wonder what the other people in that campground would think about a bag of food in the bathroom," I said. "They're probably saying, 'Oh look at those poor people with the bicycles; they don't even have a car. Maybe we should give them some money.' Meanwhile, they'll be sitting in their heated RV's, drinking hot chocolate and watching generator-powered TV, and they probably won't actually give us any money."

Geoff laughed. "Why would you want to spend all of your vacation in a portable little room? What's even the point of traveling if you're just going to drive around and watch TV? They're the ones I feel bad for."

"I wouldn't mind a portable little room and a TV," I said.

We crossed the last city street and entered the campground at the end of town. All around us, generators hummed amid the yellow outdoor lights and lighted windows of motorhomes and trailers. My and Geoff's campsite was quiet and dark — just a small tent and two bicycles leaning against trees, all covered in a fresh coat of snow.

I brushed the powder off my rear panniers and began to unpack my clothing. There was a sadness to the scene, a hint of poverty, no matter how temporary, to the notion of living with nothing more than the things you can transport under your own power. A little bit of the day's rain had seeped into my bag. I set aside the wet clothing on top and assessed what I had left that I could use to survive the night — a T-shirt, two pairs of bike shorts and socks. The street clothes I was wearing were already damp; my jacket was soaked. A small shiver moved up my spine. I really was skirting a narrow margin of comfort, and there were still a fair number of hours left to wait out the stillness of the night. I quickly grabbed my dry clothes and sprinted toward the tent. Geoff was brushing snow off the rain fly.

"Did it stay dry inside?" I asked him.

"Yeah," he said. "There's a little moisture on the floor. I think it was just condensation that broke off under the snow. I don't think the tent's leaking."

I unzipped the door and crawled inside. The cold, damp air from outside felt even colder where it became trapped inside the wet tent. I lay my last dry clothes carefully on top of my sleeping bag while noting every small puddle. If any more moisture gets in, I thought, all hope is lost. I really will end up sleeping in a bathroom. And then what? Get up in the morning? Put back on my wet clothes? Hop on my bike and ride to colder temperatures and higher elevations just to make it over the next pass? There was no easy escape by bicycle.

I walked to the bathroom to brush my teeth and returned to the tent just as the snowfall was beginning to taper off. Patches of clear sky had broken through the clouds, shimmering with the light of a thousand stars. Behind them was bright blur of the Milky Way, a light-wash of stars behind stars behind stars. I craned my neck at the emerging light show and marveled about how far I was from everything, how far I had traveled, all on a bicycle.

That was becoming a recurring theme for me on my first bicycle tour — the awe of distance. I'd stop for a breather on the side of the road and look back, look all the way to the horizon, and realize I had ridden across that entire stretch of land and beyond. As Geoff and I pedaled away from Moab, the desert dissolved into the mountains, which dropped into the river valley, which climbed to the far-away town of Telluride. I felt my way over every contour, devouring every slow mile of scenery until simple blades of grass and weather-worn billboards became beautiful pieces of art, forever burned in my memory. All along the highways were places I had driven through but never before seen; towns I had stopped in but never before explored. Bicycle travel was slow enough to mean something, simple enough to be possible, and hard enough to be worth it.

The first day of our trip turned out to be a particularly hard day of bicycling. In my short career of athletic ambition, it was possibly the hardest day of physical activity I had ever embarked on. We left Moab at 3 p.m. with a goal of covering 30 or 35 miles of highway before dark. We never considered that our low-point location on the banks of the Colorado River gave us only room to climb, up and then down and back up the foothills that lined the La Sal Mountains.

The brutal heat of the afternoon battered our spirits as we mashed the pedals of our startlingly heavy bicycles, which Geoff and I had never bothered to load up our bicycles during all of our "practice" rides. I wheezed up the steep inclines and held my breath down the cheek-puckering drops of an endless ribbon of rolling hills.

By the time the sun dipped low on the horizon, we had pedaled 30 miles in four hours and were still several uphill miles from the first pass. I announced that I didn't think I could pedal another mile, at least not before dark. We ducked around a cattle fence and poached a camp spot in a sagebrush field. We leaned our bikes against pinion trees and collapsed into the dirt, too tired to set up the tent or even cook dinner. The sun finally broke its searing grip and the cool air of evening descended. I lay on the ground and watched the sky fade pink to purple as an army of bats swooped and dove over my head. The bugs they were chasing were invisible; all I could see was an hypnotic dance performed only for me.

After about a half hour, Geoff finally rolled out of the dirt and set up the tent. He cooked up refried beans and tortillas for dinner. I sat up long enough to eat a burrito, and then crawled into the tent. As I lay in my thin sleeping bag that first night, every muscle in my arms and legs ached. My backbone slowly became more rigid until I could no longer flex or even move from my reclined position. My butt felt like it was being stabbed by dozens of invisible hot needles through a Novocain-like numbness. But the worst pain was creeping up from the dark corners of my mind. It arose from the discouraging knowledge that I was never going to make it. I was never going to have the strength to complete a 600-mile bike tour, and it was silly to try. I dreamed up the ways I was going to break the news to Geoff in the morning.

As daylight broke on day two, I awoke to the festering remnants of my frustrations. Geoff was still snoring loudly. I opened my eyes and reluctantly started the motions of rallying my road-worn body parts to at least lift me out of bed. I stretched my legs and realized they didn't feel as heavy as they had the night before. The ache in my arms had dulled. The saddle sore on my butt had numbed.

I opened the tent and stood to greet the rose-colored light that stretched all the way across the sky. In the stillness of the morning, I let out a long, relieved sigh. I no longer felt so helpless and broken. The air was fresh and cool and I felt a new surge of energy coursing through my warm blood. I looked at my bicycle and believed I could maybe even ride it again. The night of sleep had given my body a renewal pass for at least another day of cycling. And if I could renew for two days, why not four, or 14?

And so the next few days progressed. Each one became a little easier and a little more comfortable than the day before. During the second night, we camped out in the open desert above the Dolores River. During the third night, we made our home in a stand of spruce trees near the edge of the San Juan Mountains. By day four, we had climbed all the way to Telluride, just a couple thousand feet of elevation below the high point of our trip. We spent day five waiting out a rainstorm by taking a relaxing rest day in town, anticipating the next leg of the tour — our longest climb.

The snow had slipped from the top of our tent and gathered in wet clumps on the ground by the time we woke up on the morning of day six. The storm had moved on and hints of yellow light grazed the snow-frosted tips of the highest trees on the surrounding mountains. The hum of generators was replaced by silence. The RV windows were dark. As I crawled out of the tent, my breath swirled around my face in a condensed fog. The chilled air wrapped itself around me as I groped for my coat and bike gloves, both still damp with melted snow.

I walked to my bike and breathed in the satisfaction of having survived the night with nothing more than the sparse necessities the bicycle allowed me to possess. Geoff fired up his single-burner stove and began to crack eggs into a small frying pan. The smell of butane and butter warmed the moist air. All around us, other campers snoozed in a comfort I no longer envied and an oblivion I no longer understood. Why would anyone want to see Telluride from the inside of a box when they could see it from a bicycle?

New snow coated the chiseled granite ridge that wrapped around the tiny valley. The emerging sun cast the powder coat in a soft yellow glow, until it looked like a satin curtain draped over a broken statue. We sat in the shadows of 14,000-foot mountains, coaxing half-frozen yolks out of egg shells and dreaming up schemes that would allow us to live in those shadows forever.

We gorged ourselves with grocery store luxuries and repacked our bike bags with the Spartan essentials — tuna, tortillas, chocolate and cheese, just enough condensed calorie sources to propel us to the next town. I rolled up the tent, heavy with dew, and lashed it around my back rack. A few campers were just starting to emerge from their boxes when we rolled out. We waved at them with our wet gloves. One older couple did not wave back, no doubt regarding us like the vagrants we were.

After the road veered out of town and back to the San Miguel River canyon, we met the day's first direct sunlight. It felt surprisingly hot against the morning air. Around the next curve, the big climb took hold. My breathing became deep and deliberate as I pressed harder into the pedals. Each stroke met increasing resistance, and my muscles flared and burned amid the pressure.

Climbing in Colorado, where mountain passes rise above 10,000 feet, often felt slow and endless. The false summit of one switchback only led to another, and then another, until I could not remember what it felt like to breathe normally. My lungs seared as sunscreen-laced sweat burned my eyes.

With every pedal stroke, my muscles demanded rest that I could not give them. All of my training did little to prepare me for the counterintuitive battle with my body that climbing necessitated, especially when the fight went on for hours. Just climbing into Telluride on day four, along a stretch of highway that had been carved into the side of a steep mountain, put up a demand for surrender nearly as convincing as the one I had to fight off the first night of the trip. So I went into day six prepared for the bloodiest of mind wars.

Bald, wintry peaks towered over valleys still in the throws of autumn climax. The bright primary yellows and reds of the aspen and scrub oak stood in stark contrast to the snow-coated mountains — almost cinematic in its transition from shades of gray to Technicolor. The beauty was distracting and I found myself only occasionally thinking about struggle and war, even as we pedaled past runaway truck ramps and yellow signs warning of 8 and 9 percent grades. Those were numbers steeper than any we had passed on the trip so far, but they were just numbers. And like the temperature or elevation, they started to mean less amid the sweeping big picture.

The physical realities of turning pedals also started to fade into the background. Somewhere in the back of my mind, there was still the crush of effort, the ebb and flare of knee pain, the alternating burning and numbness of a festering saddle sore. But I found myself becoming more preoccupied with my slow-moving world and everything it evoked.

Geoff was often many bicycle lengths ahead, but even when he was directly behind, the solid work of the climbs did not lend itself to banter. So I pedaled in silence and fought my fatigue through an increasingly involuntary deluge of memories. I looked at blades of grass and thought about running barefoot on the lawn as a child. I looked at the glistening fur of a road-kill raccoon and thought wistfully about my family dog, Callie, who at age 16 died earlier that year. I looked at construction signs and thought about going to warehouse punk concerts as a teenager. And as the climb wore on, my mind turned more and more inward, until there was no longer a clear distinction between the past and the present. There were moments I felt I really was running through the wet grass; or sitting in the garage with Callie after she became too old to walk much; or bashing my way through a crowd in an adrenaline-charged moment served up by a band called Gravity Kills.

All the while, my pedals still turned, until I floated back to the immediate moment only to see that everything had changed. The hemlock and spruce had become scarcely taller than my handlebars. The scraggly trees were clustered amid large open meadows of tundra and gravel. Geoff was several hundred yards ahead, a dark silhouette of a cyclist beneath the early afternoon sun. The road grade began to level off, and ahead I could see Geoff's outline start to disappear over what seemed to be a dropping horizon. Could it be? Could it really be?

When I reached that point, I could see Geoff leaning against his bike in a road pullout. To his side was a sign — "Lizard Head Pass, Elevation 10,223." The top.

"We made it. How do you feel?" he asked me.

"Pretty good," I said, and meant it. "That climb wasn't nearly as hard as I thought it would be. It's like this bike touring thing gets easier every day."

"Yeah," he said. "That was a pretty mellow climb for gaining 2,000 feet. It's all downhill from here."

"Well," I said, still aware of the 400 miles that lay ahead. "I'm guessing there are still plenty of climbs out there."

We ate a granola bar snack and took pictures amid the still-towering peaks beneath a bright blue sky. After we soaked up enough of what was at that point my most triumphant moment, we launched into the next wave: the Dolores River canyon and the Great Unknown beyond.

I locked into the descent with a new sense of urgency, furiously spinning my big ring until I reached my bike's coasting threshold at screaming speed. The new world faded quickly into the background, and with wide-eyed immediacy I only had time to think about feathering my brakes and keeping my line and not losing control. The tundra dropped into hemlock forest, which dropped into aspen groves, and the snow on the peaks was melting in the afternoon sun. My wheels spun furiously and my ears burned in the cold air until the air was no longer cold. Even at top speed, I could feel the heat of the afternoon sinking into the lower elevations.

The pavement began to level. The bike slowed. Farm fields lined the road. The downhill wave had broken. We'd surfed out an entire morning's worth of climbing in less than a half hour. Then, just like that, the work began anew. I looked back at the demise of our well-earned elevation with a sense of loss. Yet that feeling faded quickly into elation about the oncoming future.

The hard effort of cycling seemed to bring out a strange juxtaposition of past and future — as though a mind under physical stress has a tendency to bring the far in close and push the close far away. The temptation to slip into memories and dreams was strong, but I always emerged with new-found perspective. Could it be that cycling was just a reflection of life itself, or was life a reflection and cycling just another way of looking at it?

But for everything cycling could be, life itself is always fluid, in a world where everything is fleeting and nothing stays the same. The only thing I can really be certain of is the passing of time, the waves that carry me forward. And the details — the possessions I acquire, the way that I look, the places I go, the people I meet, the people I love — are too often little more than glimmers of the present in a sea of memories. Before I became a cyclist, it was all too easy for me to drift away with the tide, to become lost in the ocean, and forget that life is something that happens, not something I already have.

What I really wanted was to live at the crest of every moment — every frightening, joyful, exhausting, brilliant, mundane moment — as they passed me by. Maybe cycling, I thought, was my best means for staying afloat.

Farewell Burn, Alaska
February 28, 2008

If anyone ever made a movie about a haunted Christmas tree farm, the Farewell Burn would be a good place to film it.

I laughed out loud as I thought about psychotic clowns and hockey-mask-wearing lunatics wielding chainsaws and prowling behind the uniformly sized spruce trees that leaned into the Iditarod Trail. The narrow corridor, lined with a thick wall of twisting, snow-dusted branches, could have been the inspiration for the wintry hedge maze at the end of "The Shining." The trees were all seven feet high, just tall enough to keep a person from seeing over the top. Charred branches left over from an old forest fire rose out of the thin snow cover like skeleton arms in a graveyard.

In the descending twilight, the air was calm and so eerily silent that when my tires stopped rolling I swore I could here the "click, click, click" of the McGrath airport light, blinking on a hill many dozens of air miles distant. It was the spookiest place I had ever been. I felt so relieved, because I wasn't afraid anymore.

Long before I set out on the trail, when people asked me what I was most afraid of about my upcoming race, I would say "the Farewell Burn." This swath of charred wilderness had earned legendary status among the Iditarod mushers who raced through there. In 1978, the state's largest forest fire in history roared across the Kuskokwim River plain, burning a million and a half acres and leaving nothing but blackened moonscape in its wake.

A moonscape is what the mushers really did see in the winter, when the small amount of snow that fell on the dry area turned the Farewell Burn to an unbroken expanse of white. Where the landscape went blank, the ghost stories began. The Farewell Burn inspired numerous tales of strange happenings in the frozen night. Mushers spoke of ghostly lights where there should have only been blackness. The spirits of dead bison roamed the wasted land and dogs would stop running, lay down and refuse to move.

"Never, never go into the Farewell Burn at night," one musher wrote. After complaining about all the downed logs, obstacles he couldn't see and snags that broke his sled runners, he concluded, "plus, it's enchanted." The Farewell Burn was kind of place where people met both God and the Devil, and often sold their souls to both.

The eerie quiet hovered around me like fog, even as the night's darkness revealed a clear sky punctured by millions of stars. I strained my mind to draw a straight line between fantasy and reality. I had been racing for four days, unintentionally living on a starvation diet and rarely stopping long enough to let my heart rate drop below 100. The lines between the real world and the landscape of my mind had already been deeply blurred, and spirit bison and psychotic clowns did not seem outside the realm of possibility. I may have even welcomed them, actually, because they, along with the classic horror films they evoked, would have been one connection I had to the world I left behind.

In the Farewell Burn, amid thousands of identical trees growing up from the snow-covered ash, all I really had was myself and my distorted, somewhat macabre view of the landscape. But I was pedaling my bike over the flat expanse at a respectable 6 mph, feeling the cool air relieve some of the "heat" of the day, and turning pedals so lightly that my sore hip didn't even murmur. And so, for the first time since I left Rohn in a single-minded push to simply move my battered body and shattered mind down the trail, I could think about something other than myself.

So I thought about Geoff. When I first heard he quit the race, I reacted selfishly. "What about me?" I had thought. "I need him out here with me." It didn't occur to me that it must have been a really hard decision for him to make. He must have really been hurting to give up on something we had both been working toward for nearly five months.

Geoff and I had planned and trained for the Iditarod Trail Invitational in the same way we did everything. We fantasized about it. We joked about it. And then it wasn't so much of a joke. And then we actually had a plan. And then we just let it melt into our lifestyle, like a new favorite TV show or a kitten. But instead of setting our DVR and changing litter boxes, Geoff was embarking on 50-mile training runs in January and I was staying up until 3 a.m. so I could ride my bicycle in the frozen silence of night.

We had strange habits, but that was how we lived our lives and that was why we lived so well together. Our goals and dreams were always deeply personal and deeply abnormal — but they almost always meshed perfectly side by side.

As I thought about Geoff dropping from the race, a noticeable chunk of my heart broke for him. Geoff had poured just as much time and money into this dream as I had, and he had turned back when I couldn't force myself to do so ... even though just being done with the race was arguably the thing I wanted most in the world.

I thought of Geoff waiting for me back in Anchorage. He had probably had taken a warm shower and eaten a big, hot meal, and he was settling into a soft couch to watch something on TV or maybe read a book. It all seemed so incredibly ideal. Did I want those things? I couldn't tell. My hip burned and my stomach gurgled and I was probably tired, probably really tired. I couldn't tell any more. I couldn't tell real from fantasy, or physical stress from mental fatigue. And I was alone in the darkness in a region more remote than any I had ever visited, or even imagined I would ever visit, and it was cold, probably really cold. I couldn't tell any more.

But for all of the surreal images and pain, all of the struggle and sadness, would I have given it all up in that moment for a warm shower and a night in front of the TV, knowing I could never go back? And I was certain then, even then, that I would not. There was something pulling me toward McGrath that I could no longer explain and no longer deny; something that had probably been pulling be toward the tiny rural Alaska town since I first looked at a Susitna 100 brochure in November 2005; something that had been pulling me toward McGrath since Geoff first asked me if I wanted to move to Alaska; something that had been pulling me toward McGrath since a cold winter day back in December 2000, when my friend Anna called me up and asked me if I wanted to take a last-minute trip to visit her friends in New York. And through that ever-widening expanse of space and time, I felt like I was moving closer to Geoff, even as I pedaled farther away.

As the night thickened, the haunted Christmas-tree lot thinned out. The shadows of trees were larger and more scattered again, twisting with the pain of decades of struggle in an enchanted wasteland. The wildfire must have spared that section, though as the true nature of the Kuskokwim River valley began to emerge in the dim light of the moon, I wondered if that was a good thing.

Clumps of dry grass rolled away from windswept, frozen swamps. Only a handful of spruce trees thrived; most were stunted and bent. The land was drier than the driest desert — all of its water locked away, unobtainable in the ice and snow. This was not a horror movie. This was not purposeful evil. This was harsh indifference, and I remembered why I had reason to be fearful.

Across the open swamps, I could see waves of green light lapping the low rolling hillsides of the northern horizon. In four nights on the Iditarod Trail, I had seen the northern lights three times, but never paid much attention until that night. The green glow danced and shimmered, casting bluish reflections on the snow as straighter streaks of white shot through the sky like meteorites. I had never before realized that the Northern Lights were not a static entity, but light waves in a constant state of flux. One minute, the entire sky would be cast in green. The next, dark and streaked in crimson.

For dozens of feet, I gazed at the sky, watching the patterns of light reach toward me and retreat, taking on the shape of trees and animals — the spirits of spruce and bison. When I looked back down at the trail, it was ever unchanging, moving in a straight line toward the single marker of civilization I had: the blinking FAA light over McGrath in the distance. So I looked up, to the constantly fluctuating colors in the sky, putting on the kind of show no human could ever create.

Then there was darkness for a while — a period I have no memory of. The northern lights may have still been dancing. The FAA light may have still been blinking. But I was slipping away, without warning, again. I heard a loud screech just before I tumbled forward into a cold blast of powder. A snow bank surrounded my body as I looked up, startled. Suddenly alert, I concluded that I must have slammed on my brakes before I crashed my bike. But how did I crash my bike? Had I been looking up at the sky?

I glanced up again. The northern lights were quiet. The sky was sparkling with new stars. I swam out of the snow, righted my bike, and looked around. I needed to focus. I dug in my backpack for my mP3 player. I had learned earlier in the race that it consumed AAA batteries with reckless abandon, and I did not have many to burn, so I stopped using it after the second day. But at that point, times were desperate. I resolved to use one battery, which would give me about two hours of music, just to get me back on track.

The sounds of civilization filled my ears as I settled back into the pedaling. Music told me stories about trips to Garden Grove and the fields of Athenry. All of the lyrics pounding in my ears felt unnaturally out of place, but they did help me feel more awake. They also made me feel lonely again. They reminded me of all of the times I had been shattered in the past four days, longing for some semblance of normalcy. I began to sink back into despair.

The moods on the Iditarod Trail are fickle, and they swing so wildly in such a short period of time that any civilized psychiatrist would probably diagnose them as manic depression. I already knew that huge mood swings were just the way of the Trail, but I should have known that the huge high I was feeling at the top of Bison Camp would not be enough to get me through the night.

I looked at my GPS and figured I had traveled about 20 miles in four hours. I had 25 more to ride into Nikolai, and no reason to believe that trail conditions were going to deteriorate, which worked out to five hours of pedaling. That would put me into the village at about 3 a.m. It amounted to a 24-hour day, but things could be worse, I thought. I could handle it. The Dropkick Murphys and Jimmy Eat World screamed in my ears, and I turned up the music louder.

My headlamp flickered and I stopped to change the batteries, pulling the last three out of my backpack. My battery supply really was getting low, but I was

GHOST TRAILS

sure I had some reserves in my frame bag. I followed my dull yellow spotlight along a straight line of snowmobile and bicycle tracks. The Northern Lights were gone. The slog had set in.

I crossed over a large open stream that someone had actually built a wooden bridge over, which seemed a huge luxury in the wilderness. I had drank a lot more water than I anticipated since leaving Bison Camp, and I knew my water supply was getting pretty low again. The stream, Sullivan Creek, provided a quick source of water, but it was too far down to reach from the bridge. I was too frightened to dip my bottle into the creek from the uneven snow banks, which I was certain would collapse underneath me.

I stood on the bridge for several minutes, mulling my options. I only had five more hours into Nikolai, about 16 ounces of partially frozen water in my bottle, and another 32 ounces in my Camelbak bladder. It would probably be enough. And if not, I could always pull out my stove to melt snow. I took one more wistful glance at the creek and continued down the trail.

I had probably pedaled no more than a mile from the creek when I felt cold powder blast me in the face, again. I did not hear a screech before I hit the snow. I had not even bothered to squeeze the brakes. I had simply tipped off the trail.

I crawled out from the bank and shook the snow from my face, trying to stop my head from spinning. What was going on? I shined my headlamp around to locate any obstacle I might have hit. The trail was as flat and straight as it had been all evening. My tire tracks simply veered off to the side and into the snow. That could only mean one thing — I was falling asleep on my bike.

The adrenaline surge from crashing my bike recharged my alertness, and I got back on the saddle and tried to pedal faster. I had to get to Nikolai as quickly as I could. My body was no longer cooperating with my mind. Another half mile went by and the adrenaline wore off, my mind began to dull again, and I woke up once more in the powder.

"This can't happen every half mile all the way to Nikolai," I thought. But what if it did? I had tried all my options — my mP3 player was blaring, my standby adrenaline was flaring out as fast as newspaper in a forest fire, and my caffeine pills were in Rohn. Should I just get back on the bike and continue riding and hope I don't fall asleep into a tree or an open stream? If I were driving in that kind of physical state, that would be a really bad plan. If I were driving in that state, I would have no choice but to pull over.

I looked in disgust at the bivy bundle strapped to my bike. Did I really have to resort to that again? I felt like I had taken a ton of rest in Rohn, but not really. I had been awake most of that time, stewing in my fears and fretting about the future. And I had a huge meal in Bison Camp — but not really. It was 1,500 calories at the most, and it had been about the only food I had eaten all day. I scolded myself as I unhooked the bundle and began digging a trench off the side of the trail.

"You brought this on yourself," I said out loud. "This is your fault."

But I was more alert than I had been on Rainy Pass, so I made an effort to better set up my camp of desperation. I propped my bike next to the trench to help block the cold breeze that was already kicking up. I put on my down booties and grabbed half of a chocolate bar to take into the bag with me so I could enjoy a "warm" breakfast. I made sure to stuff my water bottle at the foot of my bag so it wouldn't freeze. I thought about sleeping with my Camelbak, but I did not like the idea of having that ice baby pressed against my chest. So I simply filled up my water bottle with some of the water inside the bladder.

"32 ounces will be enough until Nikolai," I thought. I left the backpack outside in the cold.

Just as I was settling in and drifting off to sleep, I heard wheels rolling up the trail. Wheels that could only belong to Bill and Kathi.

"Please, please don't let them see me," I hoped against hope. I was right next to the trail. I had my reflector-covered bike propped up mere feet from it. I had purposely done that so travelers would know I was all right, but I didn't want those travelers to be Bill and Kathi. I didn't want them to see me in my weakest moment, failing miserably at the race. I did not want them to know I was scared.

"Jill?" Bill called out. "Jill?"

I sputtered a bit and tried to sound like I had already been asleep for a while. "Wha? Yeah?"

"Are you all right?" Bill said.

"Yeah, yeah, I'm great," I said. "I was just really tired. I was falling asleep on my bike, so I decided to take a nap. I'm going to get up in a couple hours and start going again."

"So you're OK?" Bill sounded uncertain, but it was one of his virtues to give even the most inexperienced rookies the benefit of the doubt.

"Yeah," I said. "I'm great. Just tired."

"OK," he said. "I'm really sorry to have woken you up, but I had to check."

"And I'm really glad you did," I said. "Thank you."

And with that, I listened to Bill and Kathi's tires roll away until I was alone again with the silence. I started to wonder if I really was all that tired. Maybe that last spill into the snow was all the jolt I needed to get me to Nikolai. But I had taken all that time to unpack, and I did feel pretty good taking a break in the warm humidity of my sleeping bag. It wasn't so bad in there. I could hang out for 20 minutes or so. I hugged my chocolate bar and the set of maps I had been reading, and thought about how comforting a cobweb-filled haunted house and the company of ghosts might be as I drifted to sleep.

Mount Sukakpak, Alaska
June 8, 2003

"You know," **Geoff said** as he shifted through the meager contents of our bear-proof canister, "now that I think about it, when I was planning the food, I was really thinking about packing for two people more than four."

He pulled out dried beans in a small plastic bag and a half dozen tortillas.

"Some of these tortillas were supposed to be for lunch tomorrow. But ... we can each have one small burrito tonight, and then we'll divide up the last two tortillas and the cheese for the hike out."

Jen, Chris and I stood around him like orphans around the gruel pot, quietly dumbstruck. What was Geoff saying about rationing food? Who rations food? Storm-bound mountaineers ration food. Aboriginal hunters ration food. Four friends on a relaxed, two-night backpacking trip in the Brooks Range of Alaska stuff packs full of gourmet couscous and granola and eat themselves silly. We do not ration food.

But it was starting to look like our small spaghetti dinner the night before and single-tortilla lunch was not going to absolve itself during dinner. We had been hosting big packs through the trailless tundra, slogging over tussocks and across rivers, and we were hungry — ravenous — and single-track-mindedly so. We wanted one thing and one thing only, and that was the one thing we could not have. Food. I thought about all of the times I had eaten reduced-sugar yogurt and reduced-fat potato chips and wished I could have all of those calories back. Geoff's crash-diet announcement might well have been the worst news in the world, although, in all honesty, none of us had heard about any of the other news in the rest of the world for more than a week.

Chris, stoic as always, just shook his head and looked down the Bettles River. "At least it's only about five miles, maybe six or seven back to the van," he said.

"Are you sure that's it?" I asked, already feeling the jitters creeping in. All alone in the wilderness and out of food. What could be worse?

"Pretty sure," Chris said. "We just follow this river to the confluence, and then we can hike along the Koyukuk all the way to the bridge."

"So it's all pretty level?"

"Should be," Chris said. "Maybe there's some gravel bars we can walk on."

"Well, tell me when you guys want to make dinner," Jen said, sounding bored. She walked to her tent and crawled inside. I glared in her direction. This wasn't an emergency, but it was a genuine situation, and she wasn't even concerned.

I looked to Chris, who was starting to gather sticks for the night's fire, and Geoff, who was setting up his camp stove. I wanted to see a sign of some kind of urgency or acknowledgment that this was a crappy turn of events. But everyone was content to just go about their camp routine as though rationing food was just another in a long line of our duties on the trail.

I sighed as I grabbed our single pot and walked toward the river to collect water so we could cook our starvation ration of beans. The sun lingered in a pale blue sky over Mount Sukakpak, the 4,000-foot peak we had bagged and were attempting to circumnavigate during our first big Alaska wilderness backpacking trip. I looked at my watch. 10:30 p.m.

We had been north of the Arctic Circle for a week and didn't bother to keep track of the time anymore. The sun would continue its lazy arc downward for the rest of the evening, grazing the tips of the chiseled granite skyline around 2 a.m. before swinging gently back into a deepening blue sky. Setting was not something the sun did in this part of the world in June. And we were just starting to get used to it, even with dinnertime set sometime between 11 p.m. and midnight.

Mount Sukakpak cast a long shadow over the braided ribbons of the Bettles River. I knelt down on a gravel bar and looked north. I wondered if I drew a straight line starting from the point where I stood all the way to the North Pole, would it ever hit any remnant of human civilization? I had this hunch it would not. I also believed my imaginary line would cross through places no human had ever set foot in. The world north was still as untrammeled and wild as it had been before any person walked on the continent. There was a surreal sense of alien distance in the idea of being so far north, a mysticism in the image of latitude as a circular stairway leading to the beginning and end of the world. Which one we were headed toward, I couldn't be certain.

Before we started our backpacking trip, we had already seen the northernmost point of our summerlong trek through Alaska: the icy surface of the Arctic Ocean where it met the shoreline of Deadhorse. We had driven a 1990 Ford Econoline Van outfitted with a custom roof and a truck bed trailer 4,000 miles from Salt Lake City to the top of the state just to see it.

It was all part of our Alaska summer, my next "once-in-a-lifetime" job-free adventure. The trip started in May 2003 with Geoff and our friends Chris and Jen. Our van, which we purchased for the trip, lumbered through Canada up the Cassiar Highway. We paused at so many bike trails, camp spots and fishing lakes along the way that it had taken us a month just to reach the Alaska border at its northernmost east-west highway. We rolled through Fairbanks and continued driving north on the pothole-peppered Dalton Highway, trying to push our rattling van "all the way to Prudhoe Bay."

We discovered that Arctic Alaska and the North Slope were still locked in winter in early June. We shivered in our tents at night. The air temperature was right around 35 when walked onto the thick ice of the Arctic Ocean.

"No polar bear swims for you guys," our tour guide told us jokingly as we stood over the frozen sea. But I felt like we had been polar bear living for the better part of the month. The farther north we drove, the longer late winter lingered — like we had been running away from the onset of spring in our relentless pursuit of latitude.

We left Prudhoe Bay to retrace our wheel tracks back down the Dalton Highway and tour the southern half of the state. Turning back south was a strange sensation, like we were turning our backs on all of the thousands of miles we had driven and hiked and cooked and slept and argued our way through just to reach that northernmost point. The fact that there were no more roads or even land north of that point forced our hand, but it still felt wrong. Even more strange was the idea of letting go of winter after so long. But just as soon as we started driving back down the Dalton Highway, spring came.

Almost overnight, the drab brown tussocks and wilted grass of the tundra erupted into a blaze of green grass shoots and pink and white flowers. Even where patches of crusted snow clung to the ground, seedlings bloomed around the frozen edges and lent the landscape the bright contrast and color of a patchwork quilt. The caribou herds that we before had mostly seen only at great distances were starting to move closer to the road, munching on the grass and seedlings with the urgency of an animal that knows the all-you-can-eat buffet is only open two months out of the year. Small birds fluttered among the tussocks and the omnipresent white ptarmigans were suddenly mottled with new patches of brown feathers. We started to become excited about spring and the prospect of even more new life as we drove further south.

The backpack trip was Geoff's idea. He wanted a chance to really see the Brooks Range. And to him, backpacking was the only way to get out into the heart of a wilderness where wilderness was still true, and not some contrived woodland shaped by the National Park Service.

We had been driving up and down the largely uninhabited Dalton Highway for the better part of the week. I already felt a little wilderness weary, and I mostly saw the backpacking trip as an unneeded delay of our return to real human civilization when what I wanted most was a cold Pepsi and a big tub of ice cream. But I conceded that it would be silly to drive right through the Brooks Range and not even venture inside. So Geoff planned a mellow three-day trek around one of the most popular peaks in the area.

"Yeah," the ranger in Coldfoot had told us, "probably 20, maybe 25 people go up there every season."

So we drove our van to a bridge across the Koyukuk River and parked on a gravel bar next to the clear-flowing water. We packed up our overnight backpacks with clothing, sleeping bags and Geoff's misjudged meal plan, which had been cobbled together from the food we had left over after living out of our van for a week. Three days worth of food for four people, and Geoff managed to pack it all in a small bear-proof container the ranger had rented out to us.

We took our first tentative steps across the lumpy tundra, rolling our ankles on the tussocks and stumbling through bogs as we began our ascent of Mount Sukakpak. I found no excitement in the act of hiking where there was no established route. I wheezed beneath my loaded pack and trailed my friends until the four of us had fanned out across the mountainside, each stomping our own path through thin stands of stunted spruce. I was in back and had no idea if I was even walking the same direction my friends were, but I assumed "up the mountain" was a correct course. I stewed with irritation about Geoff, who was so in love with the idea of forging through the wilderness that he couldn't even wait up for me.

The slope climbed above tree line and the tundra gave way to smooth talus. On the open rock, I made out the figures of my friends. Chris and Geoff were small silhouettes in the distance and Jen had drifted a ways down the ridge, although she was still parallel with me in altitude. When we finally converged on the spine, it was agreed that we would put our packs down and climb to the peak. I put my pack down and sat on top of it.

"I'll wait here for you guys," I said. I rifled through the top pocket of my pack until I found the book I had been carrying. At the time, hiking only seemed necessary to maintain forward motion for the duration of our trek. When forward motion wasn't required, I was going to sit back, relax and dream of Fairbanks and ice cream.

"You're not going to climb to the top?" Geoff asked.

"No," I said. "No, I'm not."

Geoff, Chris and Jen dropped their packs and started up the peak. I sat in the heatless sun on a barren patch of gravel for nearly two hours while my friends climbed to the top of Mount Sukakpak. When they returned to the ridge, they showed me a glut of new digital camera photos of marmots and purple clumps of wildflowers and sharp gray peaks rippling toward distant horizons.

"You can see forever," Chris said. "If it wasn't for that oil pipeline, there'd be no signs of people as far as you can see. It's really cool."

I mustered a smile. I wanted to see humans. I wanted to see the oil pipeline. I wanted to see some sign of the routine life we had left so far behind just to lumber through the northern half of the continent with nothing to do but see.

The four of us picked up our packs and began to make our way down the ridge to the other side of Sukakpak.

Below the mountain, narrow strands of the Bettles River braided through a wide gravel plain. Surrounding it were the gothic spruce trees and alder branches that were just beginning to bud with the first leaves of spring. As we descended, I noticed that the sprigs of green emerging from the tussocks weren't nearly as far along as they had been on the south side of the mountain. We were north-facing now, in a region still clinging to winter.

We gathered on the shore of the river late that first evening and broke camp. Geoff cooked up a pasta dinner that seemed small, but no one complained. The next day, we stayed in camp and explored the area. Despite my ambitions to sit around and do nothing, I did make it out for a day hike with Geoff. That evening, we watched a lone caribou battle its way across the ribbons of the rushing river. It seemed to be charging directly toward us, like it was trying to intimidate us. The caribou straddled two gravel bars only a few dozen feet from our camp spot and stared us down. When we showed no sign of moving, it finally turned around and swam back to the other side of the river. I wondered how many humans that caribou had seen. I wondered if we were the first humans it had ever seen. I pulled out my book and read by the light of the high June sun, filtered dimly through the safety of my tent.

By dinner time the second night, it had become clear that we had nearly eaten ourselves out of food. We cooked up our severely meager burrito dinner — I doubted there were 500 calories in the thin wrap — and rationed out a small bag of oatmeal, half a tortilla, and a couple ounces of cheese for the following day. Geoff and Chris insisted the third day would be short and it wasn't more than a half day's hike back to the car, even going all the way around the mountain rather than up and over it as we had on day one.

"No climbing," Geoff said. "It'll be a breeze."

But the acid hunger was starting to burn my stomach by the time I woke up the following morning. The small serving of oatmeal did little to soothe it. I folded my small tortilla-and-cheese wrap in a baggie and stuffed my lunch in the top of my pack.

I filtered a small amount of water from the Bettles River, enough to tide me over until lunch time, the gave the filter back to Geoff so he could carry it. We set out along the gravel bars until the shoreline narrowed and the forest squeezed in. After that, we started bushwhacking through a thick web of alder branches further up the mountain, which hacked our pace down to an excruciating creep. And all the while, the line of the Bettles River kept drifting farther north. I watched the facing mountains creep closer to us as the shadow of Sukakpak slipped further away.

"Uh, shouldn't we be turning south by now?" I said.

"We shouldn't be too far from the confluence," Chris said.

Long minutes went by, and then an hour went by, and still our northwest progress continued. Finally, Chris suggested we cut back over the ridge and connect with the Koyukuk downstream.

I looked up at the looming ridge on the other side of Sukakpak. The top was at least 1,000 feet of climbing or more just to reach its low point, and the thought of more climbing made my empty stomach churn. It was already nearly noon and we were still miles from the van. The hottest day of the summer so far was bearing down. It was easily 75 degrees in the shade. As we crossed boggy meadows in the direct sun, it felt like 90.

I started sucking the dregs of water from my Camelbak. I thought about asking Geoff to stop and lend me the water filter so I could collect some more, but he and Chris were already far away, cutting a direct line up the ridge. I wanted no part in that push, so I veered diagonal with Jen, hoping to find the gentler path up the mountain. Even Jen walked faster than I felt like moving, so within minutes of making our decision to abandon the river, I was alone again.

The trees had shortened and thinned and I was walking on the hard gravel of real elevation when I first saw it, sparkling chrome and drawing a clean line through the craggy wilderness — the trans-Alaska oil pipeline. The steel channel paralleled the highway, mostly above ground, for the entire distance between Fairbanks and Prudhoe Bay. Where there was chrome, I thought, there was road.

And where there was road, there was a way home. My enthusiasm surged and I veered due west, making a direct line toward it, back down the mountain. I wouldn't have to climb any more once I dropped to the Koyukuk River, I thought. I would just walk the flat, smooth gravel bars and keep my eyes closely locked on the pipeline and its ultimate prize — the bridge back to the road.

I pushed my way through the thick vegetation until I could see chunks of ice rushing through gray water. But before I could reach the river, I met the lip of a sheer cliff. It dropped directly into the current, more than 20 feet below my feet. There was no way to walk beside the river, only through the thick vegetation I had hacked through to reach the water. I had not thought before about the possibility of paralleling the river in the Arctic jungle all the way back to camp. It didn't seem possible.

All around me were alder tangles, grabby little branches that clung to my clothes and pack and trapped me in place until I thrashed and swore my way free. That effort would gain me a foot, maybe two, of real ground before I'd have to do it all over again. I thought about going back up the ridge, but it seemed too far to climb. I couldn't face the climb again. Not on the account of my own overeager stupidity. But that's when they found me.

They were just specks at first, minor stings to add to the slashing twigs that already were drawing plenty of blood. But then they started to swarm, biting deeper and more zealously. I was lost in a black cloud by the time I realized I was being attacked by hundreds of baby mosquitoes.

It was as though they had just hatched an hour before and decided I was the only source of blood for a dozen miles. Perhaps I was the only source of blood for a dozen miles. I screamed with every ounce of volume available in my scratchy breath, but the baby mosquitoes were not scared.

I wrestled out of my pack, still snagged on alder branches, and dug through a pocket until I found my bug spray. I wielded it skyward and sprayed and sprayed like I was firing a machine gun into a cloud of smoke. Then I pointed my only weapon at myself, coating my skin and hair and mouth and eyes in a solid coat of pure toxic bug repellent. It burned like acid where the mosquitoes had already clamped down. It blinded me and filled my throat with fire, but it was the only relief I had known since we left camp that morning. The mosquitoes scattered and left me alone, with my detached pack still hanging from the bushes, fresh blood dripping from scratches on my arms and the Koyukuk River rushing effortlessly beside me.

I looked across the swift current at the oil pipeline, with its chrome glistening in the sun. It was so close I could almost reach out and touch it, and so far that I might as well have been sitting in the heart of the humanless wildernesses that Chris and Geoff were so drawn to. I shook my pack free from the branches and strapped it back on my shoulders. I looked into the murky water, choked with clumps of ice and glacial silt, and wondered if my pack could float.

How quick and painless it could be to just jump in the water and swim to the other side, to the side with the pipeline and the road. I might end up far down-stream, but that would be a good thing. It would get me closer to the van. The water would be cold, but submersion short-lived — hopefully — and it was such a hot day. I watched the river flow beside me. I imagined myself inside of it. Common sense of rationality had been drained out of me. All that I had left was an overwhelming desire for swift relief from the horrible wilderness — the kind of swift relief offered only by the instant release of the river. Or death.

Was death really one of my options? I shook my head, rattling loose my last threads of intelligence and survival instinct. Of course death wasn't an option, but it certainly was a possibility. The ice water was flowing fast and I was with-out a life jacket. The current could drag me under just as easily as it could carry me to the other side. And if I did make it to the other side, would I even man-aged to crawl out before I succumbed to hypothermia? The Koyukuk River cer-tainly did not care either way. And the only way to find out would be to accept the swift release of death as possible if not likely.

I did not want release that bad after all. I hung my head and began the slow, obstructed battle back to the high country.

By the time I reached tree line, I was spending less time thinking about the oil pipeline and the horrors of the Koyukuk jungle, and more time thinking about my cheese tortilla. It was the last portion of food I had with me. I had no idea where I was or if I was even going to reach the van any time soon, and it seemed reckless to devour my last source of calories so quickly. I decided I would hold on to it until I was certain I was within sprinting distance of the van, and then I would eat it, and then I would eat everything inside the van.

The afternoon marched on with me. Sweat released searing streams of bug spray into my eyes as my empty stomach gurgled with thick acid. My throat was scratchy and my mouth dry. I had been out of water for the better part of two hours, but still didn't think about that as much as my hunger. Thirsty I had been before. Hunger was a whole new experience.

It was late afternoon when I finally saw my salvation, the maroon roof of our junky old van, sitting alone on the side of the road. I had not seen Geoff, Chris or Jen since we inadvertently split up hours before. I had no idea how far I was behind them, but I was beginning to suspect I was quite late. I was annoyed that Geoff never came back to look for me, never waited for me, never worried about me. Why did he always think I was just like him, happy to be left to my own devises, left to the whims and uncaring will of nature? Maybe he just didn't understand how truly unkind these places were to me, or how exponentially the empty space between us grew when we were surrounded by wilderness.

It was already the summer of 2003. Geoff and I had traveled the continent together, and explored some of the more remote regions of Utah and Colorado for the better part of two years. And yet, somehow, we always ended up in the same spot. I had no reason to believe Alaska would be any different.

I pulled out my cheese tortilla and ate it joylessly as I descended to the van and the suddenly smooth, gravel-lined shore of the Koyukuk. Geoff, Chris and Jen were already gathered around our folding table and a smorgasbord of lunch food. I looked at my watch. It was 6:30 in the evening.

The tiny mosquitoes zoned in on my sweat streaks and began the buffet anew. I stopped several feet short of my friends to apply a new coat of bug spray. I tossed my pack in the dirt and walked up to the table. As I stuffed whole stacks of Pringles in my mouth, Geoff said, "We were beginning to wonder where you were."

"I made a bad choice about dropping to the river," I said. "I had to go all the way back up the ridge."

"I did that, too," Jen said.

Chris swatted his arm. "Man, the mosquitoes just erupted," he said. "Can you believe that?"

"I can," I said. "Spring comes real fast in the Arctic."

"And goes fast, too," Chris said. "Two more months and it'll be snowing again up here."

"Maybe we should come back then," Jen said with a mouth half full of a bite of her thick veggie sandwich.

"We'll be down in Southeast Alaska by then," Chris said. "But we still have Denali and the Alaska Range. We should plan a longer trip through there. We could put something together with maps."

Geoff and Chris started strategizing possible routes as Jen and I stuffed our faces in silence. The food did not taste as good as I hoped, or satisfy as much as

I anticipated. It went down like so much more dead weight, settling over a sour pit in my stomach that could not stop digging. The wilderness was relentless and cruel. Why couldn't they see that?

Fairbanks was still days away. Anchorage was likely another month by the time we made it through the lure of Denali and yet more mountain wilderness, free of humans as far as the eye could see. Then it would be another month or more before we would roll back toward Salt Lake, back to my old life and possibly my old job and a sense that even a summer in Alaska would change nothing about who I was. After all, Salt Lake was a place I felt I could not occupy without establishing conventional boundaries and settling down. And the one person I wanted to share that space with was incapable of doing either.

Farewell Burn, Alaska
February 29, 2008

Something died in my sleeping bag as I slept. I was sure of it.

There was a fleeting panic that I was the thing that had died, but then, how could I have a sense of smell if I was dead?

Surrounding me in the total darkness of my sleeping bag cocoon was a piercing odor so fluid I felt like I was swimming through it. It was the smell of rotting seaweed, and spawned-out chum salmon, and a landfill baking in the August sun. I reached for my headlamp and shined the beam toward my feet. I half expected to find a dead mouse or a rotten porcupine carcass lying next to me.

But all I could see was the rumpled mass of polyester and nylon that circled my body. It was the clothing I had been wearing, without removing once, for four and a half days straight. The surface was clammy and damp from my warm breaths that had been circulating inside the tiny space for more than three hours. I pulled my knees toward me face, drew a deep breath, and coughed. My tights emitted a funk unlike any funk I had ever experienced that close and personal. The funk was all over me. The funk was me. I was the thing that smelled like death. And I didn't feel much better.

I coughed a few more times before I rolled onto my stomach and started the now-all-too-routine "sleeping bag" chores. I gathered up my maps that were crumpled at the head of the bag and studied them one last time just in case the 25 miles I had left to pedal into Nikolai and somehow magically turned to 20 or 15. Then I force fed myself breakfast — half a chocolate bar, of which I only had one half left. My appetite was so stifled that it didn't even matter I was trying to stuff down food amid the salty sweet stench of the ages. It went down the same — horribly — either way.

I wadded up the wrapper and stuffed it in another corner of the bag while I reached down toward my feet to find my water bottle. While I slept, I had kicked it all the way to the end of my bag. I had to dig through the seldom-used fleece foot folds just to find it. As I wrapped my fingers around the bottle, the soft plastic did not give at all. It felt as hard as ice. And as I pulled it into the beam of my headlamp, I realized with a sickening pang even worse than the stench that the water was ice.

My 32 ounces of water had frozen. Solid. Inside my sleeping bag. As I slept on my sleeping pad curled in a little ball, my water bottle rested atop the snow at the end of my bag, far away from my body heat, with only a layer of nylon and down to protect it from whatever ungodly cold air was circulating outside. That layer hadn't been enough. I wrenched off the cap and flicked my tongue at the solid mass inside, unable to gather even a drop of water. I was thirsty. And I remembered, with sinking regret, that I had left my Camelbak outside.

I slowly opened my sleeping bag and rose to a furnace blast of frigid air. My watch told me it was 2:30 a.m., though that hardly seemed to matter. It seemed like it was perpetually the middle of the night in this race. I grabbed at my down coat and mittens, which were stuffed at the head of my bag. I took deep gulping breaths as I crammed my clammy, stinky body into even more layers to steel myself against the cold. When I had bundled as well as I could bundle up, I knelt into the snow and groped for my Camelbak. The entire backpack was coated in a thick layer of white frost. The material was as stiff and frozen as though someone had coated it in hard glue. I shook the pack violently, listening for liquid, and heard nothing. I tried to open the bladder but could not make the frozen lid turn. All was as expected, and worse than I could have feared.

I stood back up and limped to my bike, which was also coated in thick frost. The zipper of the frame bag refused to budge. I had to take off my mitten and clasp the searing cold metal with my bare fingers just to force it through the ice shield. My torso started to shake and my shoulders convulsed. My teeth chattered wildly. I knew I had to start moving quickly. But even as my mind raced and muscles shook, every other part of my body moved as slow as molasses.

I grabbed a handful of chemical heat packs and tore them open. The warmers inside were as solid as blocks of ice, and just as cold. I rubbed them between my mittens but nothing happened. They were as frozen and useless as my water. I tried to start rolling up my sleeping bag, but my body was so wracked with chills I could hardly control my arms. My thermometer dangled outside my Camelbak and I did not dare — DID NOT DARE — look at it. Even though I expected it to simply be bottomed out at 20 below, I was almost worried I would see some-

thing gruesome, like the mercury crashing out of the bottom of the thermometer and dripping blood-crimson mercury onto my fingers.

I tried to roll up my sleeping bag again, but my extremities were becoming
more chilled and useless by the minute. What should I do? I fretted and shivered.
I could run around until I warmed up. I could simply abandon my bike and my
sleeping bag and sprint all the way to Nikolai. Or I could crawl back into my bag
with my chemical heat packs and water, try to thaw them out, and get out at a
later time, when I was better prepared.

I happily chose option number three. I wriggled back into the sleeping bag
and cinched it up to the point of cutting off the air flow. The horrible stench was
still in there. I gathered my frozen belongings around me, shivering violently until
the down cocoon finally began to gather my body heat and warm the tiny climate
zone surrounding me. My muscles calmed. My breathing slowed down. I drifted
in and out of sleep, always resolved to try again ... soon.

It was about 5 a.m. when I made my next real attempt. The deep sub-zero air
stabbed at me and I felt completely helpless to fight back. It wasn't that I was ill
prepared for it. I had everything I needed to keep me warm as long as I was moving. It was the transition from not moving to moving that I couldn't push
through, and even with my slightly warmed heat packs, I could only make my fingers move against the straps and buckles of my bivy bundle for a few seconds at
a time before I was forced to clench my fists and start again. I gave up, dejected,
a second time.

"What do I have left to lose?" I thought. "I will go back to bed and wait for
the sun." I crawled back into my bag, shivered until I stopped, and slept some
more.

My watch said 10 a.m. when I first noticed rays of light peeking through the
small opening in my bag. I groped for my water bottle and realized in my sleep I
had kicked it to the end of the bag again. Droplets of water had formed around
the outside and I licked them, but the thawing inside was nearly nonexistent, and
not obtainable without tearing apart the bottle and smashing the ice block on a
rock to reach the small bubbles of liquid within.

I crawled outside once again, this time to the bright morning, a new day. It was
Friday, February 29. Leap Year day. The day that shouldn't even exist but for a
contrived human calendar that doesn't make room for fractions. The new day
greeted me with a gust of wind so fierce it nearly knocked me off my feet.

I packed up successfully and mounted my bike, face into the wind, feeling as
crushed as ever. The sun had made morning idleness tolerable, but the wind
made the prospect of moving forward feel like a fate worse than sleeping in the
pollution of my own body odor. Flash-freezing gusts tore at my face until my
cheeks burned. I strapped on my neoprene mask and goggles until I no longer
had a square inch of skin exposed to nature.

As serious as the wind had become, my water situation seemed even more
urgent. I thought first of hiking back to Sullivan Creek, about one and a half

miles behind me. But I hadn't believed that water to be accessible the night before, with the bridge suspended high above the water line and the shore lined in unstable ice. What would I do? Rig up some kind of bucket system? I could pull out my stove and melt water, but prior experience trying to test it out in the open in much gentler winds told me I had about a 3 percent chance of actually getting the thing to light.

Somehow, I had to free the water I was already carrying. I pulled the deeply frozen bladder out of my Camelbak, unzipped my shell, coat and fleece jacket, and stuffed the bladder down my base layer shirt. Held tightly against my chest, my ice baby chilled deeper than it ever did on Rainy Pass. I gasped a few times until the cold shock sank into dull numbness. If it melted even one ounce of the water locked inside, it would be worth it.

I distributed my chemical heat backs evenly around my body and finally began to pedal for the first time in more than 12 hours. I couldn't believe how much time I had wasted out hunkered down in snow holes. Seventeen hours in Rohn. Twelve hours on the Burn. I wasn't a racer. I was a lumbering train wreck, crashing so slowly that it wasn't even clear whether I was slamming into the ground or succumbing to erosion.

Raging wind gusts tore around my hunched body. Frost formed almost instantly around my mask, and thickened with each laboring breath. My calves flexed rapidly. My quads burned and my injured hip throbbed. I could not push my speed beyond 5 mph, even at what felt like good effort atop the relatively hard-packed snow. I finally understood why the Farewell Burn was such a fearful place, and it had nothing to do with ghosts. It had everything to do with the minus-35-degree nights and 50 mph winds.

In the light of day, the eerie mystery of the Burn had been replaced by hateful nothingness. Strands of trees popped out of the snow like dandelions from cracks in a sidewalk. The clumps of "woods" were so short and thin that they did almost nothing to protect the trail from the raging wind.

Everywhere else was an open expanse of wind-swept swamps, icy streams and barren meadows. I looked everywhere for the smallest indication of flowing water and found nothing. I might as well have been in the Sahara Desert. The result was the same. But instead of burning in the heat, I was withering in the cold.

Every mile or so, I stopped to eat a few handfuls of snow and choke down one of the few foods I had left that I was willing to eat — dried cranberries. Even beyond my incapability of getting anything else down without water, I was noticing an alarming trend with my trail food habits. Everything I wanted to eat was either candy or pure sugar. My peanut butter cups went first. My chocolate went next. My cranberries were well on their way out. I had bags full of nuts, fruit and nut bars and Clif Bars that I would never consume. So much for bicycle riding promoting good health. Even though I was about 50 percent certain I was going to quit the race in Nikolai, in the back of my mind I had already resolved — should I ever lose my mind enough to enter the Iditarod Invitational again — I was packing only candy.

As the afternoon wore on, the wind picked up speed and strength. Nearly continuous gusts sandblasted the trail, coating it in drifts of fine sugar snow that were impossible to ride through.

The soft spots forced me to get off the bike and walk every few dozen yards, and the drifts were becoming deeper and more frequent.

If the trail turned even a few degrees away from the direct headwind, the crosswind gusts were sometimes so strong they would knock me right off my bike. I took at least five hard hits, falling shoulder-first into the deep powder off to the side of the trail. As I crossed large treeless swamps, I could actually hear the moan of big gusts approaching long before they reached me. I began to think of that moan as a storm siren, a warning that told me it was time to step off my bike, stoop down, put my face between my knees, and wait fearfully as the blast of frigid air steamrolled past me.

The large gusts would leave hundred-foot-high ground blizzards in their wake, rendering me blind in a snow fog until the rare lull allowed the powder to settle again. A mere two days earlier, the development of hurricane-force wind and drifted snow would have been devastating. But by the Farewell Burn, I was grizzled, trail-worn, and stoically willing to accept the perpetual injustice that was the way of the Iditarod Trail. Such was the nature of my thirst. In a world covered in water, I had nothing to drink. I greedily eyed the expanse of snow, knowing it could do nothing for me. Just like dying of thirst in an ocean.

It felt like another lifetime had passed when I was halfway to Nikolai. I had quit the race so many times in my head that I was tired of it, and I was half glad I hadn't seen another person pass by because I was genuinely worried I might just demand a piggy-back ride. Of all of the blunders one can make in the Iditarod Trail Invitational, the inability to be self sufficient is right at the top. But I was so thirsty that even drinking my own urine sounded appealing, if I had any to drink. I hadn't peed once since I left Bison Camp. I could almost feel my tongue shriveling up inside of my mouth.

I reached the abandoned fish camp I had seen on my map. Piled on the shoreline was a heap of a log cabin. It was a sad little structure, weather scoured and on the verge of collapse, but the sight of it extracted a yelp of joy from my battered enthusiasm. If I could get inside that cabin, I could get out of the wind. And if I could get out of the wind, I could get my stove to light, and I could get water.

I ran up to the structure and yanked on the door handle. The door wouldn't budge. A large pile of snow had drifted against the building and frozen in place, blocking the cabin's only entrance. I kicked and kicked at the drift and didn't even chip its surface. It was as solid as concrete. I managed to crack the door about an inch, just enough to peer inside with one eye. I could see an old camp stove, a rusty pot, even bottles of propane that may have still held fuel. Everything I needed to make water was in that cabin. All of the water I needed surrounded me. It was everywhere. And I could obtain none of it. None of it. Injustice always prevails.

As I stood next to the cabin, a small plane buzzed over my head. It doubled back in the wind and flew over again — a sure sign that the pilot was looking right at me. I lifted my arm in a small wave, hoping not to inadvertently send a distress signal. How long had I been out there? It was Friday, about 1 p.m. That would make it day five. When was the last time I had made contact with the outside world? I had ridden 165 miles in just over 36 hours, and the next 125 in whatever time followed. 125 miles? In three and a half days? That seemed absolutely awful. No wonder planes were flying over my path. They probably were looking for my body.

The plane passed by once more and I wondered if it would try to land on the river. Through the roaring wind, I could hear the plane's mosquito buzz fade into the distance and disappear. I told myself I was relieved. But really, I was disappointed.

I reached inside my coat and pulled out my ice baby, hoping against the odds that it found a way to thaw. The bladder still felt solid in my hands, but when I unscrewed the lid and tipped the opening against my chapped lips, cold, clear water came trickling out. It dripped down my throat like nectar and filled my stomach with warmth and light. There wasn't much in there ... half a cup, maybe six ounces, but it filled me with a rejuvenating blast of energy that I was certain I could ride all the way to Nikolai. I packed my ice baby back into my shirt and mounted my bike with a big smile on my face. That's always one bright side to the times when life is really hard: It doesn't take much to spur happiness.

I finally reached the town limits of Nikolai at 4 p.m. I felt like a freeze-dried version of my former self, the wind having ripped away whatever I had left of my voice, my eyes puffy and swollen and the skin on my fingers pink and raw.

I knew Nikolai was a small Alaska Bush village — communities that are typically less regulated and more impoverished than their urban counterparts. But I hadn't until that moment understood what that meant. A small cluster of weather-worn houses littered the bluff above the Kuskokwim River. Shells of vehicles and windowless sheds were strewn haphazardly among them. There was no town center or business district. The only building that looked public was a community building/school, dark and seeming shuttered at 4 p.m. on a Friday.

I experienced a few seconds of panic when I thought I might have to take refuge in an unpopulated ghost town. There was nobody outside — no cars or snowmobiles driving down the street, no children playing in their front yards, no dogs barking. It was still 10 below and blowing like a hurricane, but the emptiness in that island of human civilization was eerie.

I followed posted race signs and pedaled up the snow-packed street to a nicer, almost suburban-like house on the outskirts of town. I propped my bike in a snow drift and dawdled around uncomfortably outside until a big Alaska Native man opened the front the door and beckoned me toward him.

"You Jill?" he asked me.

"Yeah," I said.

"We've been waiting for you. I was about to go looking for you. We thought you'd be in here this morning."

"Yeah. So did I."

"But then Mike, that's the guy who did the fly-over, he said he saw you at the cabin. He said you looked good. But then you still took I while to get here."

"Yeah. It's been really windy. And I'm really slow."

"Well, glad you made it," he said, holding out his big, calloused hand. "I'm Nick."

"Jill," I said, even though he already knew my name. I couldn't think of anything else to report, so I said, "Glad to meet you." It seemed recitation of pleasantries was one of the few social skills that survived my trek through the wilderness.

"I don't know why you all come all the way out here like this, on your bicycles," he said. He pointed to a couple of snowmobiles parked in the driveway. "Now that's the only way to go," he said, and let out a big belly laugh.

A curtain of furry animal skins hung from a rack in the doorway. The somewhat stale smell of death filled the entry way, and I was sure it wasn't all me, but I didn't mind. I took off my coat and pulled the water bladder out from beneath the front of my shirt.

"I was trying to thaw it out," I explained to Nick as he gave me a confused look. He laughed.

Inside the house, the temperature was at least 80 degrees — sweltering against the outside temperature that could have easily been 100 degrees colder. It was a shocking contrast. I started stripping off layers immediately to keep from passing out from instant heat exhaustion. A TV blared at full volume in the front room. On a couch near a roaring wood stove, a little boy and a woman holding a baby stayed fixated on the screen without even acknowledging that I had walked in. Nick sat down next to them and started massaging a huge bloody skin that he had fanned out on a round table in front of the TV — like a coffee table, but used to pin down dead animals. A giant beaver, maybe, or even a coyote. I was fascinated with this culture, and I wondered if this family realized how much richness they had achieved amid the frozen wasteland.

Nick's wife stood up from the dining room table and walked toward me. "Hi, I'm Olene," she said. "We wondered if you'd make it. Would you like coffee?"

"Oh, coffee would be awesome," I said. "But could I please have some water?"

Olene led me to the kitchen and filled up Big Gulp cup with tap water. I guzzled all 32 ounces in seconds, until the sweet liquid ran down my chin and onto my shirt. I felt a rush of wellness course through my blood, lubricated at last, and let out a happy sigh of relief. Without a word, Olene took the cup and filled it again, and then filled a mug with coffee.

"You and Nick are amazingly nice," I told her.

"We like to help you," she said. "Bill and Kathi, they put us in charge of watching over the racers, and we like to help. It isn't much, but we do what we can."

"It's everything," I told her.

Olene asked me if I wanted some moose stew. "Food is expensive up here, very expensive. But we get a good moose and I can make stew. You probably won't like it, but it's good food for the racers."

"I'd love some," I said. I had never eaten moose in my life. I wasn't a red meat eater and I didn't think I'd ever start, but Olene could have offered me cat food and I would have devoured it gleefully. It wasn't really that I had my appetite back. Despite an entire day fueled on only chocolate and dried cranberries, I still didn't feel hungry. But I resolved to eat and drink everything Olene put in front of me. More than my own health and nutrition, I just wanted to take in some of the comfort of home that surrounded me.

As I spooned chunks of warm moose meat into my mouth, Olene told me about her childhood in a fish camp miles from town, how they only came into the village on occasion, but when the school opened, they moved there for good. She grew up in Nikolai, got married, had kids, helped make a life for them. But then her kids wanted to move away. All the kids wanted to move away, she said.

"We used to have more than 100 people in town, just a few years ago," she said. "Now it's less than 60. They just don't want to live here. There's not much for people here. No jobs. No money."

Jobs and money. I had those things, back in my long-ago life in Juneau. They had come to mean nothing to me as I pressed across the Farewell Burn. I would have traded them happily for the things Olene already had, comfort and warmth.

"Jill, come here, look at this!" Nick called out from his seat at a computer desk, set right next to the couch and the bloody skin. I walked up and looked over his shoulder. He pointed at a screen full of messages posted on the Iditarod Trail Invitational online forum. When I looked closer, I realized they were messages about me. As I scanned over them, I mostly saw words of concern and angst. My own mother wrote, "I know there's something wrong. I can tell something's wrong."

"See, people were worried about you!" Nick said.

A pit formed in my stomach. I did not need to know about my shaky status in the outside world.

"Do you mind if I look at the weather report?" I said.

"Um, the weather report does not come on until 5," he said.

"I mean, can I check it online?"

Nick nodded and stood up. "Read the messages," he said. "Those are good ones." I smiled at him and sat down. Nick wiped his hands on a rag and went back to working on the animal skin. I quickly flipped to a new Web screen and browsed over to the National Weather Service Web site. When I typed in "Nikolai," the screen came back with seemingly impossible figures. "*High of -4. Low of -25. Wind advisory. Southeast winds 30 mph gusting to 55 mph. Windchills to 60 below 0.*"

I sat back and took a deep breath. 60? Below? Zero?

As I checked the Weather Channel site and Weather Underground with similar results, the phone rang. Olene talked into the receiver in a quiet voice for a few moments and then walked up to me.

"It's for you," she said.

I noticed my pink, flaky fingers were shaking as I took the phone. Anyone who already knew I was there and decided to call me could not have good news.

"Hello?" I said in a crackly voice.

"Jill!" Geoff said from the other line. "How are you doing?"

"I feel good," I said. "I'm great. But how are you feeling? How's your ankle?"

"I'm fine. It's fine," Geoff said, sounding somewhat exasperated. "What's going on?"

"I'm riding my bike in the race," I said.

"Yeah, but where have you been?" His tone sounded almost angry, although it was probably just concern.

"I've been struggling," I said. "I was tired. I had to make a few bivy stops." Tears filled my eyes. I could not hold them back. "I'm doing the best that I can."

"I know, you're doing awesome," he said. "I just want to make sure everything's OK. I've been getting calls from my family, your family, oh my God — your family. I've been trying to reassure them, but I just didn't know exactly what was going on."

I explained to Geoff the process of the past few days, of Rainy Pass, and then Rohn, and then the surreal horrors of the Farewell Burn. Tears rolled down my cheeks and I tried to keep my voice from cracking. I felt like I was speaking into a confessional, begging repentance for the selfish and horrible way I had ridden the race so far.

"So now I need to hydrate," I told him. "And I'm pretty sure I'm out of batteries. I misjudged what I needed. My battery power is really low. I think I have about six hours of light left in my headlamp, maybe not even that. So I can't leave tonight because I'll run out of power and I'll be caught in the dark. I'm going to wait until early tomorrow morning, and then I'll ride into McGrath. So I don't think I'll make it until tomorrow afternoon, but I should be able to make it."

"And you're OK? You sound sick."

"Yes, I promise I'm OK. Just dehydrated, that's all."

I hung up the receiver and wished I had never heard of the Internet, never heard of the phone. More than anything, I needed Nick and Olene's house to be cut off from the outside world, to simply be an oasis of kindness in the frozen desert. The concerns and cautions did nothing but cut me down. What I needed most was comfort and warmth, but as long as I had it, I could still believe I had what it took to pedal 50 miles of flat frozen river trail. It was a task as intimidating as moving mountains.

Rochester, New York
October 22, 2004

When the sum of the effort was too much to process, I tried to think of my body and bicycle as a single machine.

I imagined my muscles, fueled by Pop Tarts and Sour Patch Kids, firing and contracting just like pistons inside an engine. The joints pulled my legs in slow, steady circles, rotating the pedals that connected to the chain that pulled the wheel that propelled us forward. If I focused on the mechanics of cycling, I told myself, and narrowed my thoughts to simple rotations and mechanical reactions, maybe my mind would fail to connect the motion to the protests from my pain receptors. Pedaling was a natural act, I told myself, as involuntary as breathing — up and down, in and out, back and forward. Everything about cycling had rhythm and flow, just like life, just like the highways that led me across the New York countryside.

The late October morning dawned gray and cold, with a light drizzle that stung like needles of ice, numbing my skin. My legs were covered in baggy rain pants, made of an industrial yellow plastic that helped complete my human-as-machine imagery. An early wave of rush hour traffic buzzed Geoff and I as we pedaled out of Rochester. I held my head down and gave every notch of available horsepower to wet pavement rotations. The weight of a 3,000-mile fatigue clung to my legs like concrete, but it was not the day to dawdle. We hoped to wrap up a two-month bicycle tour with a ten-hour, 100-mile hero push into a tiny town north of Syracuse — Geoff's hometown: Cleveland, New York.

Another person in a truck, a rude driver among thousands in the United States, pulled up behind us and laid on the horn. Geoff swore under his breath. I had long become numb to the constant threat of belligerent drivers inside American-flag-adorned vehicles. I already knew that people who loved America did not seem to love cyclists, but they never quite became murderous toward us, either.

Honking trucks were empty threats, like prank phone calls. Much more pressing were the pops and aches rippling through my knees, the numbness creeping up my fingers, and the hills that threatened to take my back-burner pain to a whole new level. I had pedaled some 3,100 miles across 11 states, and in the process, participated in enough daily exercise to rival real athletes. But instead of becoming stronger, I was breaking down.

Geoff hung on my rear wheel and prompted me to pick up the pace. "Remember, it gets dark at about 6," he said.

"I know, I know," I grumbled, seething with frustration and wishing he would just pedal ahead like he obviously wanted to and leave me alone already. He didn't seem to really believe me when I told him that the muscles in my legs were slowly wasting away to nothing, or that my knees were becoming stiff and unresponsive. We had been averaging 50 miles a day and that pace alone was killing me. We set the last day at an ambitious 100 miles because we were ready to be done with our cross-country tour. The weather forecasts were beginning to call for snow.

When we finally broke away from the last suburban arms of Rochester, I noticed that the farmland looked even drearier than the city. Thick fog shrouded the rotting remnants of long-ago harvested crops. Broken and blackened stalks rising from pale dirt gave the fields a graveyard look.

A continuous mist of rain blurred the outlines of buildings and fences. The sweet-smelling tobacco barns of the South had given way to the foul stench of pigs and cows in New York. But it was all just farmland, more farmland among thousands of miles of farmland. I had driven in a car across the United States twice, but never until I rode my bike along its back roads did I have a sense of just how rural the nation really was. I was beginning to think the whole of America was built with barb-wire fences and bales of hay.

Geoff's and my cross-country bike tour came right on the coattails of our Alaska road trip. We drove our sputtering and dying Ford van across the U.S. border out of Alberta. Less than one week later, we were packing up bulging panniers with sleeping bags and a tent and extra pairs of spandex shorts, hoping that we would find the strength to carry those items from Salt Lake City to New York. I was road-weary and training-deprived after Alaska, but Geoff and I were both still unemployed and homeless, so that moment seemed as good as any to finally fulfill my dream of riding a bicycle across the country. Our friends urged us to head out to California and dip our wheels in the Pacific Ocean, but neither of us could afford the plane ticket. So on the morning of Aug. 20, 2003 — my 24th birthday — I took the train from my parents' house to the old commune in downtown Salt Lake to begin the next trip of a lifetime.

Geoff had already packed my four panniers with the gear that would comprise everything I owned for the next two months. He added a few extra "birthday gifts" for me to carry: water bottle holders, a handlebar mirror and a new jersey. I packed the last few things I had carried with me on the train: my toothbrush, a small bottle of shampoo, and my train ticket so I would always have a memento of the last moments before I set out to become an accomplished bicycle tourist.

We wheeled our bikes to the front yard and took one last lingering look at the house we were going to leave behind. When I mounted the saddle, it was the first time I had ridden a loaded touring bike since we returned from our Moab-Colorado-Moab tour nearly a year before. The bike wavered and swayed like it had lead weights taped on the spokes. I had no recollection of just how heavy a bike became when the bare necessities of survival were lashed to it. I felt like I was trying to pedal a small tank as we made the first few strokes up the foothills.

"Holy cow, I'm out of shape," I gasped. I was already wheezing and sweating before we had even surpassed mile one.

"I wouldn't worry too much about that," Geoff said. "We're starting out slow. Just 30 miles today and maybe 30 tomorrow. You have two months to get in shape."

We merged onto Interstate 80 and began the superheated crawl up Parley's Canyon. Trucks roared by as we bounced across rumble strips and fluttered in the back draft of heavy traffic. I was having a hard time seeing where I was going — a combination of the rumble strip rattling, my sky-high heart rate, the oppressive sun and a blinding fear of the multi-ton semis that were consistently blasting us with 80 mph crosswinds. The heat of the day was an afterthought, and I didn't notice red blisters beginning to form on my legs and arms.

We limped into Park City after an "easy" 30-mile day that had taken us more than five hours to pedal. We rolled our already dusty bikes into a luxury hotel room rented by Geoff's parents, whose long-planned cross-country road trip just happened to cross paths with our spontaneous bike trip. I collapsed on a bed, convinced that I had never — even on the first day of my first bike tour — been as tired as I was at that moment.

I rolled over and stuck my face next to the air conditioner, which did little to abate the fever that was rising from my core. Geoff's mom told me my face looked really red. I peeled myself from the bed and hobbled to the mirror to take my first look at the massive sunburn that I managed to acquire that afternoon. It encompassed every inch of exposed skin. The sight was beyond discouraging. Not only had I accumulated a monstrous sunburn in just over five hours, but I also knew I would have to face the sun the next day, and the next, and the next. And not only that — I had spent what felt like all of my energy pedaling to Park City, and I knew I would have to face the pedaling the next day, and the next, and the next.

But the next day, like so many second days before, didn't seem so bad. When I crawled out of bed, I noticed I could still move all of my limbs. Nothing felt too stiff or shattered. I slathered my red-hot skin with many coats of my own sunscreen and topped it off with a final layer of Geoff's mom's SPF 50. I wrapped bandannas around my arms and pulled my street pants over my shorts. Geoff and I bid his parents goodbye and pedaled onto Highway 40 to begin the long descent into the Heber Valley.

The morning air felt crisp and cool, almost autumn-like. We ended our second day just short of the next big climb into the mountains, built a tarp shelter around our bikes and cooked a huge, luxurious dinner of vegetables supplied by a nearby grocery store in Heber. Since vegetables were heavy to carry, they were a special treat.

By day three, the long climb didn't hurt as much as I expected it to. My sunburn was starting to fade. We descended out of the mountains and found ourselves in a redrock desert that seemed a long way from home. On day four, we dodged scattered thunderstorms and rolled beneath rainbows. On day five, we crossed into Colorado. Life was good again on the bike — simple and self-sufficient.

As the sun shock and fatigue wore off, I remembered the bike's appeal, the exhilaration that drove me out there in the first place. Life on a bicycle was a life that moves in moments. Everyday life always seemed to march with a more tyrannical version of time But on a bicycle, time became distilled. Instead of seconds, I had pedal strokes. Instead of minutes, miles. Time was freer when I only owned what I can carry, and clearer when pedaling and surviving were my only jobs. A clearing in the forest, a sandy wash in the shadow of sandstone cliffs, a weathered picnic table in a city park — these places were my homes as surely as any apartment I had ever rented. And where Geoff and I moved, life moved with us, with the moment.

We left Dinosaur, Colorado, the morning of day six and began the steady climb up a treeless basin toward the heart of the Rocky Mountains. Highway 40, which in the 1960s was a major cross-country route, had long been abandoned by the Interstate system. It was home now to only a few sun-faded outposts, where the garish paint peeling off deserted motels and gunshot-riddled plastic tepees reminded the rare traveler of a road culture era long passed.

The sun pressed relentlessly on my blistered skin, and I had resorted to wearing my coat and pants even in the stagnant heat of mid-day. When I could no longer handle the coat, I tied bandannas around my neck and arms and tried to think about something besides my rising body temperature. The pavement was peppered with clumps of fur and the pungent remains of antelope and owls. When I looked up, the landscape was a sagebrush-dotted prairie strung out farther than the horizon.

We had passed through only one town that day, which to our disdain turned out to be a fully deceased ghost town. Geoff and I were both dangerously low on water by the time we reached the mountain pass we had been climbing toward all day. We rolled into a road pullout and I climbed off my bike for the first time in hours. My back was stiff and my butt throbbed where yet more tender skin had been rubbed raw.

The rest stop was strewn with rusty car frames, washing machines and other trash. Geoff pointed out a spigot that presumably tapped water, and I approached it greedily with my Camelback bladder in hand. I pumped the tap for several minutes before liquid started to gush out. It was rust-brown and smelled strongly of gasoline — a color and odor indistinguishable from the liquid that typically emerges from a gas pump. I yanked my bladder away, but it was too late — the remnants of my clear water had been fully contaminated.

I stared in disbelief at the amber sludge and finally willed myself to take a sip. It was still water, still hydration, after all. The well water tasted exactly like it smelled — unleaded fuel — and burned just as harshly in my esophagus. I spat it out and dumped the rest of the bladder's contents over the scorched earth.

"We can't drink this," I announced, looking forlornly at Geoff. "It tastes like gas." The ghost town, followed by finding nonpotable water, were horrible twists of karma. We had at least 24 miles to pedal to the next town, Maybell. It would take us three hours at the day's pace — a long way to go without water in the treeless August heat.

"I still have a little water," Geoff said. "I'll give you some." I shook my bladder dry, trying to rid it of as much contamination as I could. Geoff held his hose over the lid and dribbled a 16-ounce portion of water from his own supply. "It should be mostly downhill from here anyway," Geoff said. "This is the high elevation for the day. Since we've done nothing but climb all day, I bet there's not much to do now but drop."

My new water still tasted like gasoline, but I took comfort in the idea that I might be able to shun it if we really had a fast descent into town. We crested the pass and launched downhill, rapidly losing elevation as gravity pushed the headwind in tear-inducing gusts around our bodies. In those exhilarating moments of weightlessness, I couldn't help but feel more apprehension. We were losing elevation much quicker than we had gained it. The road grade must have been 10 or 11 percent. That couldn't possibly continue for 24 more miles.

As we whipped around a final switchback, I saw the base of a new hill, which shot several hundred feet over our heads. The road that climbed up the hill looked like a vertical wall of pavement from my first vantage point. As we bottomed out and began to climb anew, our speed dropped from 35 mph to single digits almost instantly.

"One more hill," I told myself. "One more hill."

But the top of the hill revealed yet another valley drop. We plummeted down the road and plodded back up, only to meet another. These hills weren't just rollers. They were monster rollers — climbs over entire mountains without the benefit of elevation gain or the reward of real descents. Every descent punished us with another climb. And every climb rewarded us with nothing at all.

After we had crested three of the hills and looked over the horizon to see yet another, I tossed my bike down on the pavement, sat in the dry grass, and started to cry. The unquenchable frustration had been welling up for the past six or seven miles but came out in gushing bursts. Nearly an hour had gone by since we left the pass, and we had only traveled six or seven "downhill" miles. While I sucked wind up the steep climbs, I had defiantly drank all of my water. I had believed that somehow the hill torture had to end, that physics just wouldn't allow it to go on forever. And when it didn't, I just couldn't take it anymore.

Geoff, who had put a large gap in front of me at that point, finally returned after I had been sitting in the ditch, sobbing, for several minutes. "What's wrong? What happened?" he asked breathlessly.

"I'm sorry," I blubbered. "I'm not hurt. I tried to ... but I just can't ... had to let it out. It's too hard. It's too far. It's just too far."

Geoff, to his credit, immediately recognized the seriousness of my breakdown even when he couldn't quite understand why I was so upset.

"Jill, it's OK," he said. "It'll be fine. It's only about 17 more miles. We still have a few hours of daylight. We can take it as slow as we need to."

"I'm out of water," I sobbed.

"Have some," he said, handing his Camelbak to me. "Have the rest. I don't have much left, either. But it'll be OK. We're not going to die because of a few hours without water."

"It's really hot. People get heat stroke. We just might die," I said, not really believing it, but for some reason, it felt soothing to say.

Geoff folded his arms. "So what do you want to do?" he asked. "Can you ride any more today? At all? I mean, if you want to, we can pull out the tent and camp right here, right on the side of the road. We don't have much for dinner, but I can make some tuna tortillas or something."

"Right here in the sun?" I said, feeling more deflated than ever. "With no shade? It'll be three hours before the sun goes down. And we still don't have any water."

"Exactly," Geoff said. "So if you think you can ride at all, we should probably get moving. I mean, we have three hours, but we might need that much."

I stood up and tried to brush the dust off my pants. Dirt clung to the sweat stains, and I noticed dark spots where tears had soaked into the nylon.

"Yeah, I know," I said, my voice still cracking. "I obviously can do it. I just don't want to. But I can. I just ... just had to get it out of my system. I feel better now, I promise."

The monster rollers didn't abate, and our progress continued in excruciating slowness. I pedaled the last three hours in a daze, emotionally drained and physically on auto pilot. By the time we were looking down over a last long valley — by then five miles from town and certain that Maybell was in there somewhere — the twilight had sunk too low to see much beyond the next bend of pavement.

We made it to town to find nearly everything closed. But there was a camp-ground with a shower, and a diner open until 9. I sat down at the table in my only clean clothes — my extra set of bike shorts and a jersey — and dug into a gigantic southern fried chicken dinner. It seemed like a normal thing to be doing, despite the sunburn and bike shorts. I marveled how quickly I could morph from a half-broken bicycle robot back to a real person.

After that incident — I started to refer to it in my own mind as the "Colorado Collapse" — Geoff was much quicker to offer help or a chance to rest whenever he suspected I was on the verge of another meltdown. Although we had hiked and backpacked and even completed a two-week bicycle tour before then, never before had either of us been involved in such a long period of sustained physical activity.

Geoff was a natural athlete and believed in his ability to take the strain in stride. I had always been the anti-athlete, an uncoordinated weakling who happened to have an almost unfortunate affinity for adventure and the outdoors. In my opinion, bicycling 50 miles every day pushed my body beyond anything it had been designed to do. Geoff, on the other hand, was built hard-muscled and wiry. He had traveled long distances on foot and bicycle and always knew he was capable of so much more. Backed by this psychology, Geoff treated the cross-country bicycle tour as a relaxing diversion from the daily grind. For me, it was a whole new level of daily grind, where every day seemed to promise more hardship than the day before. Even as I marveled amid stunning new scenery and hospitality, I struggled.

But I couldn't deny that I ended each day with a unique sense of fulfillment. I had seen endless days of beauty as we drove through Alaska. I had enjoyed supreme fatigue on weekend hiking trips in Utah. But never before had I worked so hard, so consistently, just to carry the day. The forward progress at the end of each evening was a tangible reward.

As the widely uninhabited high desert of the Rocky Mountains gave way to the sparsely populated Great Plains, Geoff and I started setting up our camps in town parks. I would sit on picnic tables listening to the soft spray of sprinklers as the sun set over corn fields, rippling in the wind like waves in a golden ocean. Even though I had never visited the Midwest, I continued to feel comfortably at home.

By the time we reached Missouri, though, I felt storm-weary from living outside under the constant threat of tornadoes, and road-weary from a five-month span in which I never resided at "home" more than two nights at a time. The fact that my legs could still turn pedals became a minor victory. My knees started to throb in the night. My back felt like it was developing a permanent hunch. I started to think more and more each night about New York, about the end, about "home" and what it really meant to me after five months en route.

The nights became colder as we crossed into Kentucky and the month of October. We woke up many mornings to a tent coated in frost. I was still using the same gear that I had so fearfully relied on during that one snowy night in Telluride. It was old gear by then a bit worn, and even as I shivered in the mornings, I now trusted it completely. In fact, I was learning that I could trust my gear even more than I could trust my body, because at least my gear was capable of doing to same thing day after day. My body, on the other hand, had started waking up in the mornings with stiff joints and tired muscles and a sinking suspicion that sometimes willpower alone is not enough.

The hills of Ohio nearly broke me. I did not hide that fact from Geoff as I melted off my bike and began the head-down march on foot near the top of nearly every big climb.

"This is so much worse than the mountains," I said. "These rollers, the constant up and down. My knees can't take it. I do want to keep going to New York, I do. Maybe it will take me until December to get there, but I'm going to walk whenever I need to."

"That's fine," Geoff said, and he motored up the hill to wait for me at the top.

The Allegheny Mountains of Pennsylvania were a welcome relief from the climbing. We started to make our way up and down gentle canyons and passes rather than brutal hills. Fall started to emerge in the only way it can in the Northeast — a brilliant eruption of red, orange and gold. I had never before been surrounded by so many hardwood trees, and never before seen such an explosion of natural color. The warm hues and cool air restored my vision of cycling as I thought it should be, moving with the moment and loving the place I was at, not the place I was going. So there was almost a certain sadness that carried itself as we crossed into New York, even through the elation that we had made it to our last state.

"Seems like we're really going to do this thing," Geoff said as he photographed me flexing my biceps next to the state line sign.

"We're not there yet," I said.

We swung around the Finger Lakes of central New York and camped that night beneath snow flurries in a nearly deserted state park campground. We built a fire but shivered anyway. The cold was starting to press down, and I knew for however many miles I might still have left in my clunker of a body, I certainly did not have the stamina for many more frigid nights. So as soon as the finish line was in tossing range — 100 miles, almost exactly — Geoff proposed we wrap it up.

"A century?" I said. That classic cycling term left a bitter aftertaste when I said it out loud. "I've never ridden 100 miles in one shot before. Not fresh, not tired, not loaded, not unloaded ... never."

"If we leave right at sunrise, we'll have 10 hours before dark," Geoff said. "That's about our pace. We should be fine."

"We won't be able to stop," I said. "At all."

"So what do you want to do?" Geoff asked. "Ride 50 miles and camp one more night? Sleep out in the rain when you could be bundled up in front of a warm fire?"

And I had to admit, despite my rekindled love of pedaling, still what I wanted most in my life was to be done. My mind could still appreciate movement in the moment. My body was ready to stand still.

It must have been that desire to be done that shut my energy down sooner than usual on the last day. The struggle started in full force before we had even pedaled 20 miles. We stopped at a gas station for second breakfast and choked down some Pop Tarts and a Honey Bun as we rolled down the pavement. Before that day, every meal, every snack had been a lingering and relieving break. Eating on the go was a new concept to me, and I didn't like it. It made me realize that stopping had always been one of my great joys in bicycle touring.

I had just passed mile 50 when I realized Geoff was no longer right on my wheel. The way he usually hung right behind me, wordlessly shadowing my every slow-moving stroke, made me crazy. But having him far behind me was disconcerting, too. I waited. And waited. And after about 20 minutes, I started to ride backward. On the last day of the bike trip, riding backward was a feeling even worse than the idea of losing Geoff, but what choice did I have? A driver pulled up and asked me if I was a friend of a broken-down bicyclist a couple of miles back. I said I probably was. The driver gave me a ride two miles back down the road to where Geoff was fiddling with his rear derailleur.

"My shifter cable snapped," Geoff told me. "I can only use my front gears."

He concluded he could still ride his bike, but the setback cost nearly a full hour of daylight. It also promised to delay his forward motion for the rest of the trip. "We'll never make it to Cleveland by dark," I said.

Geoff nodded. "Probably not."

"Maybe, maybe we could call your parents," I said, half joking, but half hopeful.

"That would be stupid," Geoff said. "Coming all this way just to quit 50 miles from the end."

"Well, it was just an arbitrary goal," I said. "Like, when we left Salt Lake, that's all we said, 'hey, let's bike to your parents' house.' It was just ... kind of a place to end our trip. It's not the only place we could end our trip. There are lots of places we could have decided to end this trip."

"Well, it would be really stupid to end it here, wherever this is," he said.

"It's 50 miles from where you grew up," I said. "You don't know the name of the town?"

"Why would I?" Geoff said. "There are hundreds of towns exactly like this, in every direction. We're on the East Coast now."

"Anyway," I said, "It doesn't change the fact we don't have the daylight to make it to your town. So what do you suggest?"

"I've got friends outside Cleveland, for miles," he said. "We'll get as far as we're going to get."

The dreary day just became grayer and colder as we pushed desperately into the afternoon. I felt like a back-of-the-pack cyclist sprinting to the end of a losing race. It seemed like every injury I had acquired over the course of two months — my stiff knees, my sore butt, my aching back and mushy legs — flared up in full force all at once. But my heart was beating so fast that I rarely had the presence of mind to focus on specific ailments. I could only feel one thing: Hurt.

Geoff, despite his minimalist gearing, stayed behind me without any issue, and often spoke up to tell me about an experience he had in the area as a cross-country runner in high school, or to point out the neighborhoods of his old friends and girls he dated. Geoff was beginning to recognize places. This was a good thing. This meant we were close. And yet the more he clung to my rear wheel without even a hint of hardship or struggle, the more I felt like I was the one being left behind.

Twilight set in deep when we were about 20 miles from Geoff's childhood home. He reset our destination for our friend Jen's parents' house, 17 miles from the finish at mile 83.6. Geoff asked me if I was disappointed about not logging my first century during my first big bicycle tour. I said "no," and meant it. The trip had long ago stopped being about the numbers or the distance. Sometimes I lost myself to the abstractions of pain, and sometimes I became caught up in the misplaced glory of shallow goals, but the moment, the present moment, always mattered.

The next day we woke up to full-on snow. Geoff's parents begged him to let them come pick us up, but we both said "no," and meant it. We had fought hard for those last 17 miles, and we were going to ride them. My crank groaned and creaked and chain lube no longer seemed to shut it up. My brake pads were worn to nearly nothing. Geoff had three gears and a rear pannier that was falling apart at the seams. Our skinny tires cut dark lines through the snow-dusted pavement. I just put my head down and pedaled with everything I had left.

Seventeen miles passed in less than 80 minutes — for us, flying. As we pulled into the driveway, Geoff's mom ran out of the front door, sobbing.

"You made it! You made it!" she cried. "I never thought you would!"

"I just talked to you from the Gebhardts," Geoff said. "This morning. 17 miles away."

"I know," his mom cried. She wrapped her arms around Geoff and swung him around like a small child. "I know."

I crawled off my bike for the final time after 65 days and 3,200 miles. I realized that I would not have to sit on that bike saddle again — ever — unless I for some reason chose to. I was done. Truly done. I looked up at the swirling snow and wondered what I would possibly do with my life now that I had ridden a bicycle across the country. My body was a half-broken shell of what it once had been, but I had done it. And accomplishing something as difficult as a cross-country bicycle trip made me feel like I could do anything. Anything at all.

Nikolai, Alaska
March 1, 2008

Nick showed me to a room that belonged to one of his children who had moved away.

It was mostly empty, except for a stack of boxes and a bare mattress pushed in a corner.

"You leaving soon?" he asked.

"I don't think I'll leave until 4 a.m.," I replied.

"That late, huh?"

"I only have enough batteries to keep my headlight running for about six hours," I explained. "Maybe even just four. But that should give me just enough light to make it until dawn."

I half hoped Nick would offer to sell me batteries, so I could just leave right then and get the whole terrifying run into McGrath over with. But my overpowering hopes silently begged him to say nothing so I'd be forced to stay.

"Probably a good idea," he said. "Wind's blowing too hard. May die down in the morning."

"This wind," I said. "I've never felt anything like it. I'm not even sure I'm prepared. What do you wear to travel in this type of weather?"

"I don't travel in this type of weather."

"Oh," I said. Nick — the wizened local, the Alaska Native man who had lived in Nikolai all his life, who probably dealt with frostbite as casually and frequently as people in the Lower 48 deal with sunburns — did not travel in this type of weather.

My stomach, already rubbed raw by five days of trail food and fear, felt like it was twisting around itself. At the pre-race meeting, veteran racers had told me that once I got to Nikolai I would start "smelling the barn" and being so excited to finish that the final run over the Kuskokwim River would feel like an easy coast into McGrath. But all I could think about was the wind howling like a hurricane outside and the possibility of 60 below 0 windchills that had been forecast on the Internet. I wondered whether Nick and Olene might be interested in adopting a new 28-year-old daughter. Nick could teach me to tan animal skins and I could live happily forever next to their wood stove. How was I ever going to drag myself away from that place?

I spread out my sleeping bag over the mattress and laid on top of it. Wind rattled the windows and I shivered even though the temperature in the room was near sweltering. Sleep came in fits and lulls. I woke up an uncountable number of times in the night, covered in beads of sweat and so thirsty I could hardly breathe. I drank quart after quart of electrolyte-laced water, only to wake up 20 minutes later with an urge to pee. In between trips to the bathroom, I picked at the remains on the dinner table — dried out pieces of white bread and spoonfuls of jam. Anything to get down a few calories that were at least unfrozen, if not warm.

Finally, at about 3 a.m., I couldn't take the limbo any more. The house was starting to fill up with other racers. I counted three skiers and a walker who had finally caught up to me. They grunted and coughed loudly as they stomped around just outside my bedroom door. I was so tired of the sleepless days and endless nights that even a painful slog alone in the cold sounded more appealing than another hour of that unsettling waiting game. It was the same restless sentiment that pushed me out of Rohn, but it helped me get back on the trail once before. Restlessness, not ambition, was the only emotion that was keeping me in the race. I started to pack up for what I hoped would be the last time.

On my way out the door, I stopped to sign myself out of the race checkpoint and donate to the moose stew and firewood fund. I wrote my name and time out next to Bill and Kathi, who had left Nikolai nearly 24 hours before. Next to the clipboard sat a box of Snickers Bars. I eyed them greedily. Were those for racers? They had to be. But what if they weren't? I really didn't want to steal from Nick and Olene. I reached for them but pulled away. I felt like a toddler on the verge of a tantrum in the grocery store checkout line. I wanted candy and I didn't care. I threw an extra $20 bill in the donation jar, grabbed two and stuck them in my coat pocket. Those would be a special treat for later.

I thought I had become more accustomed to the raw shock of stepping out into the cold. Like jumping into a glacial lake or tearing off a Band-aid, it hurt just a little bit less every time I did it.

But when I stepped out into the 4 a.m. darkness of Saturday, March 1, no amount of numbness could shield me from the morning's icy death grip. The wind blew so violently that it rattled loose parts on my bicycle while it sat still. What parts on my bicycle had come loose, I did not know and did not care. My fabric bags had frozen as stiff as hard plastic and I was glad I did not have much to pack up. Before I had put my goggles and face mask on, I accidentally turned to face the full brunt of the wind. My eyes involuntarily clamped shut as the gust tore through me, searing my cheeks and nose as surely as a blast of fire.

"This is insane," I thought. "If the trail is anything like yesterday, or worse, completely unridable, it could take me 24 hours to push into McGrath. I can't survive 24 more minutes out here, let alone 24 more hours. And I don't have the daylight. I don't have the nightlight." I took a few labored breaths and tried to gulp down the panic. "I'll ride two miles," I told myself, out loud, in the most soothing voice I could mange. "Just two miles. If it takes an hour, if it still feels awful, I'll turn around."

I started pedaling down the road under the sickly yellow light of flickering street lamps. The wind blew hard at my side, causing me to overcompensate my steering and swerve all over the packed snow like a drunken snowmobiler. When the street ended, the continuing trail quickly veered back onto the river. Based on the compass in my GPS, the wide corridor seemed to travel almost back the way I came. The wind pushed forcefully at my back, even though it hadn't changed direction since the day before — when it blew right into my face.

"This isn't right," I thought. I turned around and circled through town again, looking for another way out. I found the trail I had followed coming in. It formed a V off the new trail and continued in what looked like nearly the same direction — but it was definitely not the same trail. I turned back and rolled a little way down the river until I saw a sign that both assuaged and stoked my fears:

"McGrath, 50 miles" it read, but then continued, "Warning. Wilderness travel. Weather can change quickly and without warning. Travel at own risk."

"If the weather changes quickly," I said out loud, "it could only be for the better. How could it get much worse?"

The river trail flowed downstream as an otherworldly tailwind carried me almost effortlessly with it. I flew over well-packed snowmobile tracks like a jockey trying to control — but not discourage — an overeager horse. My odometer was hitting double digits for the first time since day one — 11 mph, and the 13, and then 15. I was traveling so fast that two miles came and went without me even realizing it. And I was feeling surprisingly warm inside my stacks of layers — my own little portable climate zone. Not a speck of skin was exposed to the air. Not a drop of sweat was forming on my body. I was a self-contained engine on a runaway bike, and nothing could stop me now.

I thought about a radio interview I had listened to before the race, about the human desire to venture close to death in order to feel alive. The notion of living on the precipice of death had made sense to me earlier, but didn't resonate as much in the reality of deadly surroundings. I didn't feel close to death at all. I had never stopped believing that death was close by, sure, but I couldn't feel it lurking. In truth, I had never felt further from death. I was riding through a 60-below wind chill over a frozen river in some Godforsaken part of Alaska, with warm blood coursing through my veins and adrenaline feeding happy thoughts into my brain, which was remarkably still functioning and even marginally coherent. I was a bubble of life rocketing through a galaxy of death, and I hadn't burst yet. Because of that, I felt indestructible.

"Road" signs marked my progress along the river, and I was knocking them off fast. I extracted a huge surge of energy from each one. At the 45-mile marker, I let out a loud whoop. At 40 miles, I blinked in disbelief. At 35 miles, I laughed out loud. At 30 miles, I stopped to take my first break and look at my watch. 6 a.m. It was only 6 a.m.!

Guessing that I had left the house at about 4, I acknowledged with some astonishment that I had traveled 20 miles in two hours. If I ramped it up, I could be to McGrath by dawn! And I might actually achieve a sub-six-day finish ... which was not awful. Not awful at all! Had I really achieved such a relaxed state of mind that I was actually thinking about the race again? That was almost harder for me to believe than the speed I was making.

I reached into my pocket to pull out my "breakfast" — a celebration Snickers Bar. I set it to my teeth carefully, certain I would probably have to stick the frozen brick in my mouth for several minutes before it thawed enough to chew. But as I bit into the thin chocolate coating, the nougat inside shattered into a hundred shards. Some of the pieces slid down my throat. Others rained down on my bike and gear like sugary dust. I held my mitten up to catch the shrapnel as I bit down again, then licked the chocolate shards and nougat dust off the sleeve of my coat. Snickers Bars plus two hours of deep freezing equaled shattery goodness. I decided it was my most satisfying meal of the trip.

A few more miles down the trail, my butt, which had been subject to an odd tingling sensation since mile marker 40, went completely numb. It wasn't a saddle sore, because it seemed to encompass my entire lower back. Every time I sat down on my bike seat, I felt like I was sitting on a block of dry ice. Standing on the pedals exposed the raw surface of my rear end to the brunt of the wind. Either way, my butt felt like it was slipping into the deep freeze itself.

The sensation perplexed me. I had planned for the contingent of toe, finger and facial frostbite. But butt frostbite? Who gets frostbite on their butt? I didn't even know what I could do about it. I was wearing all of the lower-body clothing layers I had. But then I remembered: I still had a few chemical heat packs stowed away. I dug around in my frame bag and found three. I rubbed them vigorously for several minutes before stuffing two down my pants against each chilled cheek. I placed the last one right between my legs to take the edge off the frozen seat. When I sat down again, a warm pillow of air swirled around my nether regions. I congratulated myself for my resilience and brilliance — a woman prepared for the worst Alaska could dish out, impervious to ice and cold.

The windblown snow drifts across the trail were becoming deeper and wider, and I started to pedal harder just to punch through them. A few grabbed my front wheel like a sand trap and stopped the bike before I could break through, tossing my body into the snow. Despite the increased risk of going over the handlebars, I continued to hit every drift at full speed. I had crashed so many times during the race that I was becoming impervious to crashes, and by that point, almost anything seemed better than getting of the bike and walking.

After a couple more hours went by, the sun rose low and cold over a spruce-studded horizon. My pace dropped considerably as the snow drifts thickened with each passing mile. Soon walking became necessary, and then frequent. Just like the day before, I found myself pedaling 100 yards and walking 100 more before I could get back on the bike and pedal again — a seemingly endless cycle.

Only by then the drifts were deep and long enough to completely obscure the trail. I could no longer distinguish the trail's line from the flat expanse of frozen river surrounding it. Despite my failing battery power, I kept my headlamp on well after dawn just to pick out the reflective trail markers.

By the time full daylight spread over the river, I was exclusively walking. I had worried I'd run into more drifting — windy as it still was — and yet I had somehow let myself believe I could make a five-hour run to the finish line. In light of how high and fast I had felt that morning, this latest injustice of the Iditarod Trail was extreme. That it could very well be the last injustice gave me no comfort. For all of the horrible punishments I could have anticipated that morning, I did not expect the Iditarod Trail to sentence me to pushing my bike the last 25 miles into McGrath.

9 a.m. came and went before I had reached mile marker 20, if it existed. I slogged through the fine power snow at a pace of about 2 mph, if I was lucky. I cursed myself for not conserving batteries for my headlamp. I had no reason to doubt that I had at least 10 hours of walking ahead of me, which would put my finishing time well after dark. The effort was similar to wading through an endless bowl of sugar — a lumpy, grainy surface with no solid ground underneath to even gain solid footing. At first I could occasionally see the half-buried footprints and faded tire tracks of Kathi, Bill and the Italian cyclist, all who had moved through there only 24 hours earlier. But by the time I came through, the windblown snow had drifted in so deep that I could see no evidence of them at all. In fact, except for the wooden stakes that marked the trail, there was no real evidence that anyone had ever set foot or wheel on that trail before.

The wind continued to blast my back, which I found infuriating. Not only did the gusts make walking more technical, but they also reminded me of everything I had lost, everything I had taken for granted only hours earlier. I reached into my feed bag to eat one of the last fruit leathers in the mix. I tore off the package with my teeth and accidentally lost the wrapper into the wind. It fluttered and coasted down the very path I was working so hard to follow. I watched it continue on its way, moving faster than I could even dream about, dancing effortlessly until it disappeared from view.

"That candy wrapper will make it to McGrath before I do," I thought. "And it's just not fair."

I started to lose track of the trail. The wooden stake markers were just too far apart, and there was no other track or berm to help me distinguish the shallow drifts over the trail from the deep snow that covered the rest of the river. The river's surface was as smooth and blank as a sheet of paper.

Every few steps I would venture off the packed trail into waist-deep snow. My heavy bike would tip on top of my body and press against my chest and head. To break free, I'd have to push it with all of my upper-body strength until it tipped away from my body so I could thrash my way out. The powder swims were more exhausting than anything I had ever experienced. Each time I fell over, another mile's worth of energy would be wasted. To make matters worse, the river occasionally curved away from the tailwind. Any strong crosswind gust would blast me into another battle through waist-high snow.

The hours that dragged by were as inconsequential as minutes, but the time lapse felt like days. The once wide-open river plain began to dig deeper into the landscape, and the Kuskokwim's banks were lined with towering bluffs. I'd fixate on a spruce tree hanging from the top of one of the cliffs and just stare at it, unflinchingly, until I finally lost focus. Then I'd look away for a while, zone out and let my mind wander, only to look up again, many minutes or a half hour later, and realize the tree looked as though it hadn't moved a millimeter closer. The slowness of The Push was stifling.

The harder I worked, the more I felt like I was standing still. I was a sprinter locked in a slow-motion dream, a slow-motion dream set in a blank white landscape, and I knew if I didn't do something different, soon, I was going to completely lose my mind.

Then I remembered I still had my iPod shuffle buried in one of my pockets. My other mP3 player needed batteries to run, and those were long gone. But I carried the iPod for emergencies. I doubted its internal battery would last longer than an hour in the extreme cold. But this was an emergency, and one hour of external stimulation and nine hours of silence was still better than 10 hours of silence.

I turned up the volume on the iPod, which muted the wind with a cacophony of beautiful noise from my recent if distant past. I knew the iPod was just a tiny electronic box charged with mass-produced music from people I had never met and places I had never seen. But in my sleep-addled mind, so desperate to hear human voices, those songs were beautiful sermons written only for me.

They told the parables of life Outside, a heaven where I could drive my car to work and watch movies and eat cold cereal right out of the box while the rain pattered soothingly against my apartment windows. Just as I had known these joys in my pre-race existence, my iPod promised, so to could I return to them in the great hereafter. All I needed to do was keep the faith and keep moving. The songs preached a comforting message — that all things have a beginning and an end, and that this, too, would pass.

Before long, the voices on my iPod sounded like the voices inside of my head. The lyrics were the same as the thoughts that were driving me, and I began to forget they existed separate from me at all.

A quiet chorus of crickets started to chirp in the distance. It didn't even occur to me that it was still at least 20 below zero and the entire landscape was buried beneath an impenetrable shield of ice. I had been absolved of all doubt. Those crickets were real, and I felt a calm, soothing sort of comfort in their music. But then the crickets quieted down and another melody began to fill the empty space — like bells ringing through the mist — low, at first, but becoming closer. And then out of the cold wind came a subdued human voice ... sad, but certain.

"You're the one that I want ... you're a chance to take ... you're a heartbreak ... and I swore you'd never leave again ..."

I gazed down at my boots, which continued to step one in front of the other through powder as fine and white as sand on an idyllic tropical beach. The Iditarod Trail. This was everything I had wanted. These were the moments I had anticipated, prepared for, and let my life be consumed by for months ... arguably years. I never claimed to be an experienced winter ultra-endurance racer, but I put in the time. I, the quintessential non-athlete, set up a rigorous training schedule and stuck to it. I trained until everything I did felt like training.

Who goes out in a January sleet storm to ride their bicycle for 12 hours when only six of those hours are even remotely light? Who waits for the temperature to drop into the single digits so they can spend a weeknight sleeping outside in their back yard, buried in a tight sleeping bag just to see if they can in fact survive? Who spends many hundreds of dollars on gear and food and travel and entry fees just to drag themselves into the bowels of their own personal hell? I looked down at the drifted snow, the Iditarod Trail. "I did that ... all of that ... for you."

"Is this how it's gonna be? ... Is this how you wanted me? ... Broken down again ... it's almost over now ..."

Why the Iditarod Trail? What made me choose this trail out of all the trails in Alaska, out of all the trails in the world? What kind of hold did the Iditarod Trail have on me? What was I out here to experience, to learn, about myself? I had spent months studying the endurance racing doctrine — about giving up comfort to reach enlightenment, about suffering to become strong. But right there, while pushing my bike in the sugar snow, everything I had believed about cycling before started to ring false. The was no strength in forced endurance. All this trail had managed to expose was weakness after weakness.

The part of me I thought was the strongest — my willpower — had collapsed on me, again and again. And the part of me I was truly worried about — my body — coasted through the whole ordeal without the slightest injuries. In fact, my body was still strong, despite the fact I had refused to feed it, had been working it beyond anything it had ever trained for, and continuously battered it in icy crashes. Through it all, my atoms and molecules continued firing just as they always had. Trainers and coaches can talk all they want about how the only way to achieve strength is through specific focus and hard work. That rang false, too. The human body is resilient when it needs to be. My spirit was the weak one.

"I was wrong ... I've wasted on ... can't figure out ... what happened to us ..."

Broken spirit notwithstanding, the question remained ... why did I seek this trail in the first place? The Iditarod Trail Invitational was such a hard race ... so much harder than most people, including myself, could even understand. Was it delusions of grandeur? Did I really think I could count myself among the hard-core adventurers of the world?

The fact the Iditarod Trail was eating me alive was no huge surprise. I was a Mormon girl from Utah. I grew up in the suburbs and didn't even pay attention to sports and athletics, let alone participate in them. I was once scared of the dark. I was still beyond terrified of water. The people watching the race from afar had no idea who they were really cheering for. They thought I was strong, that I could keep up with the strongmen, and they were disappointed and even shocked when I couldn't.

But I was never going to keep up with the strongmen. I never had it in me. And the rest of the world almost certainly didn't understand just how divinely lucky I had been just to persevere to that point.

"I won't count on ... you any more ... I'll be all right ... don't worry about me ..."

And then there was Geoff ... Geoff had started this whole mess. Sure, the 2006 Susitna 100 was my idea. And I was the one glued to 2007 Iditarod Invitational updates and I was the one who first put my name on the 2008 roster. But it was Geoff who first talked me into quitting my comfortable job and driving all over the continent back in 2001. It was Geoff who needled me into quitting my next comfortable job and driving to Alaska. It was Geoff who coaxed me to continue turning pedals across 3,200 miles of American roads. And at the end of it all, it was Geoff who suggested we move to Alaska. And where did he lead me? There? Alone on the remote, uncaring Iditarod Trail? One of the last places in the world I needed to be or even belonged.

"Aren't you happy now? ... Got what you want? ... I wanted you ... but I'm over that now ... I'M OVER IT ..."

The music launched into a fever pitch and without even expecting to, I tossed my bike angrily into the snow. My simmering frustration boiled over. I stomped the soft trail with my weak legs and throbbing feet, kicking up clouds of white powder and screaming until my voice cracked and my throat went dry. "Where are you now? Where are you now?"

The Iditarod Trail answered nothing, did nothing, was nothing beneath a cloak of untrammeled snow. My blood coursed hot through my veins even as chunks of frost rained from my clothing.

The temper tantrum proved extremely gratifying. I picked up my bike and launched into a sprint as though I could keep that up for seven hours. A misfiring of happy hormones surged back into my bloodstream and I devoured them greedily. I did not have much positive energy left to burn and I knew it, but I was so close to the end that I could not let the ghost trail beat me.

The hours passed as minutes, the minutes as hours. I'm not sure what time it was when the signs started to appear along the snowy expanse. They were diabolical, really — false signals of hope on a seemingly unending emotional rollercoaster. I had become so distracted by my skyrocketing ascents into euphoria followed by slow-motion dips into the valleys of despair that I could no longer focus on the end. I had to invest all of my remaining energy just to get through the next valley. The end was too, too far away to even imagine.

But then came the hand-scrawled signs taped to trail markers, promising an impossibly close end to suffering. "Ultrasport ... 10 more miles!" the first read with a smiley face at the end.

Ten miles. In Juneau, that distance was a half-hour-long mellow bike ride. On the Iditarod Trail, a five-hour death march. The new trail marker signs did nothing but remind me how far I had still to go. An eternity later, I saw the nine-mile marker. I watched the eight-mile sign taunt me from the end of a long straightaway for a full 20 minutes before I finally passed it.

Shortly before the seven-mile marker, actual traffic from McGrath started to pass me on snowmobiles. Besides other racers and people manning checkpoints, I had not seen a single other person on the trail since a snowmobiler passed me just before Shell Lake on day two. To me, the face-mask-clad snowmobile drivers looked like alien inhabitants in a strange land, and they regarded me with the same sentiment.

I moved off the trail to let a snowmobile pass me when the driver pulled up beside me and slowed down.

"Bout seven more miles to town," he said. "Trail's pretty bad from here. Do you want a ride?"

I so, so wanted a ride. "Thanks, but no," I said. "It's kinda a nice day for a walk."

"OK then," he said. "Yeah, I'd say about seven more miles. Probably three or four more hours if you're walking."

"It's cool," I said. "I'm OK."

He nodded, revved up his machine, and rumbled down the river toward town. The ease of his movement filled me with envy and regret. Life was so easy for those few moments the snowmobiler was with me. And then, with a few stubborn words extracted from the nether regions of reason in my head, life became hard again.

The trail finally turned off the river and began to climb into some low rolling hills just after I passed the six-mile sign. It seemed as good a time as any for my celebration lunch. I pulled my last Snickers Bar out of my coat, stuffed as much of the candy as I could fit in my mouth and bit down into an explosion of rich, buttery sweetness. I still lost some shrapnel to the trail, but most of the calories made it down. And with that, I was out of sugar sustenance. I still had several deadweight pounds of nuts, jerky and Clif Bars in my bags.

The new inland trail moved perpendicular with the wind, and even on my feet the gusts tossed me around. I swerved and staggered and righted myself in the blasting crosswind. There was nowhere to hide and every weakness in my clothing proved it — the vents in my goggles, the frost-coated holes in my face mask. Everything funneled the arctic blasts right through my body with a deep and lingering chill.

But whenever there was a lull in the wind, I started to overheat. At one point I stopped to try to pull off my outermost balaclava. It was frozen as hard as a helmet, and it was stuck to my head. My sweat-coated, frozen hair would not release the solid mass, so I left it there.

I had not yet reached mile five when a crosswind gust slammed into the bike. I stumbled and tipped off the trail, plunging deep into a powder drift. I lay in a heap on my side, with my face pressed between my front bag and a basin of sugary snow. I let out a sigh that had become all too familiar — resigning myself to the mammoth effort I needed to expend just to swim out of those holes. I braced my legs and lifted up on the steel frame, but only managed to raise it a few inches before my arms collapsed from underneath it. The bike dropped like an overambitious bench press barbell, falling heavily back onto my body.

I winced and struggled to catch my breath as dusty snow settled around me. What if I didn't have the strength to lift my bike off of me? Was I really pinned there? There? On the Iditarod Trail? Six miles from McGrath? What if no one ever found me? What if they did? Laying in a snow drift, pinned by a bike? How completely humiliating ... and funny! I started laughing in spite of myself, laughing at the whole farce of the race, the idiotic premise and pointless struggle. I laughed until tears streamed down my face.

But then, something snapped. The tears kept coming. A flash of darkness and hopelessness worse than any I had felt yet in the past week streaked through my mind. The laughing cut out immediately like a scream in the wind. And I cried.

Gobs of warm snot flowed between my mask and mouth as my eyelashes froze shut beneath a stream of tears. I cried and cried and cried. I cried for the snowed-in trail and for the mundane slowness and for all of the ways I was incapable of wrapping this race up. I cried for my frozen water and heavy bike and burning knees and throbbing calves and piles of food I could not eat. I cried for the hard, unwarming sun and the wind and the driving cold. I cried for the distance and for my aloneness and for the remoteness and the mean, mean, unmerciful nature of it all. I cried because my adventure was nearly done. I cried because I knew I was going to survive it. I cried because I knew there was an end to the suffering. And I cried because I knew there would be no end to the drive.

My body shook until everything went silent. I realized my iPod had died at some point and I could hear the wind. It sounded so far away. I summoned every last ounce of energy still trickling through my bloodstream, and pushed up on the bike one final time.

Salt River Range, Wyoming
August 2005

"This isn't much of a trail, is it?" I said.

Geoff rustled through a stand of aspen trees and plopped down where I sat on a patch of dry grass.

"We must have lost it back there," he said, gesturing down the sagebrush-dotted slope toward the canyon we had been working so hard to climb out of. I leaned back and dug my feet into the pale dirt, releasing a cloud of dust into the bright afternoon.

"Did you see Monika?"

"She's up there, somewhere," Geoff said.

I strained my neck to look up the slope. "Monika!" I called out blandly. No one replied. "Should we go look for her?" I said in an unconcerned voice to make it clear I wasn't willing to work for any more meaningless elevation unless it was an absolute emergency.

"She'll realize we're not behind her and come back down soon enough," Geoff said.

The Salt River Range of western Wyoming loomed over us, casting stark shadows where slate-gray peaks plunged into the narrow Greys River valley. It seemed to me an odd gathering place for four old friends from four different states, none of which were Wyoming. Monika was moving away from New York City, and took a wide swing around the Rocky Mountains on her way to her new home in Michigan. Chris lived in Salt Lake City, a few miles from the university where we all met as students. I had logged 10 full months as a resident of Idaho Falls after extracting myself from an unsatisfying life in Utah. Geoff was determined to make his new home in Alaska, having spent the entire summer traveling the state for a third time.

"So what are you thinking?" Geoff asked after a few minutes of silence.

I lifted my arm and pushed my forehead into the sleeve of my shirt to mop up beads of sweat. I should have found a different place to sit than a shadeless slope beneath the August sun, but it seemed like too much work to move now.

"About Alaska?" I said. "I don't know. I guess I'm going. I guess I don't have anything to lose by it."

"Because I'm leaving either way," Geoff said. "And you should come."

"There's just so many logistics," I said. "And planning. I didn't want to think about it seriously, and now it's really crept up on me."

"You've had all summer to think about it," Geoff said.

I shrugged. I didn't have the heart to tell him that just three weeks ago I had made the decision that I was definitely staying in Idaho Falls, and I didn't care what he did. But I didn't have the heart to tell him back when I made that decision, either. I was so easy to stand on the other side of the gap when Geoff was far away. Now he was back on my side of the divide, badgering me to cross the bridge.

"I think the Homer Tribune is going to offer me a job," I said.

"Did you get the job yet?"

"Not yet," I said. "At least I don't think so. I haven't heard back." I pulled my cell phone from my pocket and looked at the blank screen. No service. There didn't seem to be cell service anywhere for miles. "But they seemed really serious. I bet the job offer's sitting in my voice mail right now."

"So then we're going to Homer?" Geoff said.

"It would seem that way."

I sighed. Going to Alaska with Geoff. I had hyped it up as a dream move when Geoff brought it up shortly after I announced I could no longer stomach life in Utah and made the move to Idaho Falls. There was a new life in Alaska — a real move, not a trip, so the possibilities for new adventure were endless. But more than that, Alaska held new promise. Geoff and I had been drifting for so long that we found it harder to connect. Maybe Alaska, I told myself, was the solid ground we needed.

But then Geoff decided he wanted to travel for a few months. I kept my paying job and let the dream stagnate and wither in the summer sun. Now I just wanted to live in Idaho and go to the gym in the mornings and sleep in my big bed next to my air conditioner, and why was Geoff still pushing for Alaska so hard? It's not like either of us had any real reason to go there.

"Well, I already have that place near Palmer," he said. "I have to put a deposit down soon, so you need to let me know pretty quickly here whether you're going

164   GHOST TRAILS

to Homer or not."

"Ah yes, the hovel," I said. "I have to say, if we move to Homer, I at least want to find a place where the bathroom and house are connected."

I heard a loud rustling of bushes and looked back again to see Monika marching toward us, lips pursed.

"Hey! Guys, I don't think this is the trail," she said. "What are you doing sitting down?"

"We don't think this is the trail either," I said. "You got ahead of us so we stopped to wait for you. We need to turn around."

"Well, fine," she said without even stopping. Geoff and I got up to follow Monika as she stomped down the hill.

"So much for that," I said.

Geoff shrugged. "It wasn't that bad."

Shortly after we returned from our failed hike, our friends Monika and Chris packed up, bid us goodbye and good luck, and drove away in two cars to return to their respective corners of the world.

Geoff and I settled in for one more night of camping near the Greys River. The cold current carried a rush of slate-colored sediment down from the high peaks. The canyon was crowned with points we had not had enough ambition to reach for, even as the weekend dragged on. It had been a quiet vacation for Geoff and I, a chance to sit in the sun and squint toward the future.

I sat at a picnic table with another book in a stream of Alaskana that I had spent the summer poring over. I had nearly cleaned out the Idaho Falls Library's northern nonfiction catalog, from dog sled racing literature to hunting humor, and all I had learned was that I knew less about Alaska than I had feared. But what I did know gave me plenty of reasons to fear — ice and grizzly bears, cold and loneliness.

The sun had settled low on the horizon when Geoff walked up to me with a handful of berries. "Look at these," he said. "Soapberries. They have these in Alaska."

"Are they any good?"

He stuck one in his mouth and spat it out. "No," he said. "They really do taste like soap. But I've heard Natives mix these with sugar and water and make some kind of dessert. Like Eskimo ice cream."

"Is that any good?" I said.

"I don't know," Geoff said. "Probably not. But we could make some and find out."

"When I move to Alaska, I'm going to spend the whole summer picking blueberries," I said. "And then you can bake some pies. I still remember how good those things were when we were up there last time."

"So that means you're coming?"

"I don't know," I said. "I'd really like to know about getting that job."

"So just check to see if they called," he said.

"Can't. No reception."

"Why don't you drive out to where you can get some reception?"

"I ... guess I could do that."

"It's not like we're doing anything important here. I'll make dinner while you're gone," he said. "So when you get back there'll be that and some soapberry surprise."

I fired up my own car, which had sat unused since the beginning of the trip, and drove away from camp, following the faint tire tracks of Monika and Chris. The nearest town was at least 25 miles away, on a rough gravel road snaking through the narrow canyon. I stopped several times but never found a cell phone signal until I was well away from the mountains, standing next to a potato field along the Idaho border.

By the return trip, my stomach rumbled with hunger. The road curved ceaselessly and I kept expecting to see Geoff's camp around the next corner, but failed to, again and again. I had only brought one CD with me for the whole trip — a homemade mix of Modest Mouse songs. I had listened to it so many times that I had it memorized all over again, so I flipped through the tracks for the one song I wanted to hear.

"You're standing by ... the grey ice water ... out in the wind, above the ground, out in the weather ..."

So, Alaska, I thought. It seemed silly to have built up so much anticipation just to talk myself out of it. But I hadn't expected Geoff to fly back down to the Lower 48, offer to drive up to Alaska with me, and all but drag me kicking and screaming from my comfortable, if a bit soft, lifestyle. He was good at that. He had always been good at that. Too good at that.

"You had yourself ... a crazy lover ... becoming frozen trying hard to forget her ..."

And what about all of the fearful parts, the things I had read about, the ice and the bears? People in my Alaska books raved about the wilderness and the winters, but how different could it be from Utah, or Idaho, or Wyoming? I had spent a whole summer in Alaska, enough time to know it really only had a few scary animals and a lot of space on the rest of the other 49 states. But all of that space was overwhelming. At the time, it felt like being hit head-on by the daily Wilderness Express. If you fell into a river in a place like the Brooks Range, you could spend days dying of hypothermia and no one would ever find your body.

"But that could happen here, too," I said out loud as I watched the fading sun cast orange streaks on the tips of the mountains. "That could happen anywhere."

"You got a job ... up in Alaska ... it's easy to save what the cannery pays cause there ain't no way to spend it."

And then there was Geoff. What would happen after I followed him to Alaska? Although Alaska was something we had both talked about, in the end, it was Geoff's idea. Was I really going to tailgate his whims for the rest of my life? There was Geoff, and then there was Alaska. Could I really separate them? Could I really say I'd ever do it if I had no one to follow, if I was by myself? At the same time, could I really say I'm doing this for him and only for him? True, if Geoff left, I'd have nothing really to hold onto in Idaho. Truth be told, I never had a strong reason to go in the first place … but yet I held on.

"You took the path of lease resistance … on the phone, cutting out, talking short to long distance."

Everyone is always so focused on the future, I thought. The idea of moving on, of moving forward, of not living in the past — it seemed to be a philosophy that most people based their lives on. But most people are so busy chasing the future, they don't realize that every second of every day, everything they do slips forever into history. The future is just an idea; the present is a flash of time, an ungraspable instant. The past is the most real thing anyone knows.

"On the arctic blast … on the arctic blast … on the arctic blast."

Twilight was in deep descent by the time I finally returned to camp. A cold pot of something starchy sat on the picnic table, along with a bowl of a bitter-smelling, red antifreeze-looking liquid that I could only assume was the soapberry surprise.

A single beam from a headlamp reflected through the top of Geoff's tent. I walked up to it, listening only to a quiet chorus of crickets punctuate the stillness in the air. Before I could unzip the door, a groggy-sounding Geoff said, "So, what'd you find out?"

"I got the job," I said.

McGrath, Alaska
March 1, 2008

I knelt down on my hands and knees in the packed snow and gasped wildly.

I tried to gulp down the last of my sobs and rush a little oxygen to my racing heart. I felt like I had just accomplished an impossible feat, like clawing my way out of a steel cage with my fingernails. And even though I knew the simple act of pushing a bicycle off of one's body shouldn't really be all that difficult, I felt fully exhausted.

My head continued to spin as I stood up, and I decided I needed more air. I reached up to remove my balaclava and hat. The fleece material was still frozen as hard as a helmet. I pulled up, but nothing happened. I yanked again, and still my head gear didn't budge. I tried to twist it around, and realized that not only were my hats frozen, and frozen together, but they also were frozen to my head. When a couple of hard pulls didn't even result in a little bit of pain, I knew that my hair must be frozen as well.

I removed my goggles and squinted at the glaring white expanse. The frozen world was creeping in, becoming a part of me, and I was already a part of it. I put my goggles and mittens back on, and bent over to pick up my bike from a drift. All around, marks of a deep struggle disrupted the otherwise smooth surface of the snow. I pulled the frame with what I thought was a reasonable amount of strength, but it didn't lift up from its overturned position. I felt tears welling up again, but I knew I had to fight them.

"You've had your allotted breakdown for the day," I said to myself in an exasperated tone. "Now pick up your damn bike."

Another Herculean pull had the bike rubber-side down and leaning against my hips. Never before in my life had six miles seemed so insurmountably far. "It's just walking," I said in that same annoyed tone. "One foot in front of the other. It's not hard."

I took my first wobbling steps through the sugar as my bike squeaked beside me. This close to town, the trail was better packed. The powder, marked with fresh snowmobile tracks, scarcely reached above my ankles. Still, when I tried to wade through it, I felt like I was walking in knee-deep snow, up a steep pitch, at about 20,000 feet elevation. Every breath was short and desperate. Could that be the total body breakdown I had been waiting for? Or was it simply my weak spirit finally winning the battle for the right to surrender?

The small signs of hope continued to crop up along the trail, increasingly less hopeful and farther apart, at least in terms of time. Five more miles. My steps crunched through the snow like a rhythm beating in the distance. My iPod, its battery nearly spent but working again after I stuffed it deeper in my clothing, continued to play music softly. I diverted my gaze from the trail repeatedly, looking for any indication of a house or a snowmobile or a person. I just wanted some glimmer of change, something to assure me I was in fact moving and not standing still. To assure me that time was still moving and not standing still.

Four more miles.

My emotional roller coaster had bottomed out in a dark valley, and I no longer had the power to climb back out. Although I had pushed through my last sobbing breakdown, and although I understood — somewhere in the back of my mind where rational thought still wandered — that four miles was not far, I was constantly on the verge of tears.

It was all the simple things now that made me want to cry. The drone of a jetliner 30,000 feet over my head ... the occasional dog print pressed into the trail ... the sun dipping low on the horizon ... the way my GPS screen told me McGrath was in the hundreds of feet, as the crow flies, from where I was standing, and still I saw nothing but spruce and snow.

"Somehow, the suffering has to end," I said, trying to soothe the dominating despair that rational thought just couldn't penetrate. "It just isn't physically possible for this to go on forever."

I would say this and then stop — mittens clasped around the handlebars, feet planted in the trail, neck tipped all the way back as my frozen hair tugged at my scalp. I would stop for no reason, draw labored breaths, and stare at the sky. The sun burned so bright it was almost white, like the trail and like the world. I thought if I could sit down, if I could just sit down for a deeply needed rest, maybe I would fade to white myself.

Three more miles.

I rounded a corner and heard the quiet but unmistakable sound of a motor. Its ragged hum was consecutively beautiful and alarming. There was a small berm in the trail. After I labored over it, gasping as though I had just climbed a mountain, I realized I was standing on a road. An actual road. It was packed with snow, but it was undoubtedly a road.

Down the street, I saw a few snow-covered roofs emerging from the forest. The hum of the motor drew closer until I saw two small children on a snowmobile drive past me. They smiled and waved. I just stared at them, wide-eyed, as though they were ghosts.

After 12 hours of drifting through my thoughts alone in the wilderness, I found it almost impossible to process the barrage of new images. I had already accepted the imagined as reality, so my mind could only assume reality was imagined. I watched the snowmobile coast over a hill and away from view. As its hum and my shock subsided, the truth began to sink in. I was on a road. A road the led to McGrath. Which meant I was going to make it!

I mounted my bicycle for the first time in more than eight hours. The wheels started to roll with gravity without any contribution from my legs. I was moving without effort. The phenomenon was astonishing: the wheels, the bicycle — what a wonderful invention. I began to rotate my feet. The wheels moved faster. Three miles was mine for the astonishingly small price of a few simple pedal strokes. And just like that, I was a bicycle racer again. I swore I would give the sprint to the finish everything I had left.

I laid into the pedals and began to coast down the snow-covered road. A small blue sedan puttered toward me. The driver waved to me and I waved back as he passed, both of us having no real sense of just how alien we looked to the other. I could feel actual sweat dripping from my ice-coated hair down my clammy forehead. I looked down at my odometer just to see how fast I was racing. The screen, cast almost black in the cold, flickered at 8 mph. I shifted up to my big chainring — the first time I had done so in the race — and laid into the pedals again. The odometer ticked up to 9 mph before falling back to 8. 8 mph. That was all I had to give.

But even at 8 mph, three miles passed by in what by then seemed like a blink in time. When I coasted up to a home with the terminal sign outside —"Alaska Ultrasport" in red block letters — I still hadn't come to acceptance about an actual end to the race. I stopped a few yards up the road and just stared for several seconds at that sign.

The dormant racer in my head was fired to near full throttle again. "You're in a race!," it screamed at me "You finished! Seconds are ticking away. Go inside and sign in!" But a larger part of me just wasn't sure whether or not I was ready to face to real world. The struggle of the past six days had broken me, surely, and made me appreciate the mundane comforts of life in ways I never expected. But like a battered dog facing release from its captor, the cold indifference of the Iditarod Trail had become all that I knew, and I was reluctant to leave it.

I finally willed myself to roll my bike toward the house. A thick plume of wood smoke rose from the chimney of a rustic-looking two-story structure. There were at least a half dozen other bikes parked outside — and surely at least that many people inside the house. I took a deep breath. Was it really just 12 hours before that I had left the warm glow of Nick and Olene's house? It felt like a lifetime. I set my bike against a snow drift, tiptoed up the stairs, and knocked on the door.

"You made it!" Kathi exclaimed from her perch on a comfy-looking couch. The warmth of the wood stove swirled around, a sensation almost as shocking as the blast of cold air had been early that morning. Two strangers, a man and a woman, were working feverously in the kitchen. The man rushed toward me and ushered me inside the doorway.

"Come in! Come in!" he practically shouted in a thick German accent. "How do you feel? You look cold. Are you cold?" I shook my head. "Good," he said. "Make yourself at home! Take your shoes off. Take your coat and hat off! Relax!"

He plopped me down on a rocking chair just a few inches from the doorway. I lifted my stiff, numb hands and tried to contemplate the bewildering puzzle of where to begin. I moved to take off my hat, but it was still frozen to my head. I leaned over and began to wrestle with my boots. The effort was terrible. They felt frozen to my feet. So I began trying to unzip my outermost coat. Nothing was happening. My fingers felt like they were coated in hard rubber, and I couldn't summon the strength just to pull down on the zipper. So I stood up and yanked as hard as I could at my hat. It tore free from my hair in a shower of ice.

Kathi laughed. "We looked like that we were got here, too."

"When did you guys get here?" I asked.

"Early this morning," she said. "It took forever to get here. Boy, those snow drifts were awful, weren't they? How long did it take you?"

"I have no idea," I said. "What time is it?"

Kathi looked at her watch. "It's 4:25. You finished about five minutes ago. 4:20. Pretty good. Almost broke six days."

"Six days," I said quietly to myself. "Has it really only been six days?" I began working on my coat zipper again.

"So I guess if it's 4:20, it took me just over 12 hours to get here," I said. "Pretty awful, huh? I honestly believed I could do it in five."

"So did we," Bill said as he walked in from an adjacent room. "We were riding that tailwind, just giggling about it, but then all that snow had drifted in. Then we were like, well, time for a nice walk." Bill seemed so matter-of-fact about everything in the race. Nothing was ever hard to him. Just different.

"How bad was it when you went through?" Kathi asked.

"I couldn't see the trail," I said. "I couldn't even see your or Bill's tracks."

I sat down and finally succeeded in pulling off my boots. Then I started peeling off my socks, setting everything in a damp pile next to the door. It felt awkward and almost wrong — the process of permanently removing my layers. Like peeling off pieces of dead skin.

"Well, you have a smile on your face, so I guess you had a good race," Bill said.

"Well, a lot of that smile is just happy to be done," I croaked. My voice was becoming more and more hoarse, as though it had atrophied over days of silence and could no longer operate for more than a few sentences.

"Did you hear about Ann?" Kathi asked.

"Ann?" I said. "Runner Ann? No. What happened?"

"She froze her eyes," Kathi said solemnly.

"Wait, she what?"

"She froze her eyes," Kathi said again. "She was just outside of Nikolai when it happened. Nick had to go out on a snowmachine and rescue her. They flew her to a clinic here and then she flew out to Anchorage just a few hours ago. They think she's going to be fine."

"She's going to be OK?"

"Yes, now," Kathi said. "She was blinded out there on the trail. The cyclist Alesandro found her. He helped her zip up her coat. He put her in her sleeping bag and biked to get help. He probably saved her life."

"How ... how did she freeze her eyes?"

"She wasn't wearing goggles," Kathi said. "And running right into the wind."

"When did it happen?"

"Early this morning," Kathi said. "Sometime before dawn. I thought you might have still been in Nikolai when Alesandro came to get Nick."

"I must have just missed them," I said. "Wow. I hope she's all right."

"The people at the clinic here think she's going to make a full recovery," Kathi said. "They were able to fly her to the hospital in Anchorage really fast."

I leaned into the chair and let out a long sigh. I couldn't shake the thought that Ann and I were out there at the same time, fighting the same wind. She was facing it. I was riding away from it. What if our positions had been switched? Could it have just as easily been me? I imagined her groping around, blinded, struggling to find her sleeping bag or even zip up her coat. And to have that happen when she was all alone? A chill moved down my spine. We were all so fragile, and all wandering so close to the edge. Even the slightest changes in our situation could easily leave us shattered. I had plodded into McGrath on a wave of grace, and I hadn't even realized it.

"It's been a busy day," the German man said as he peered inside the oven. "But you're lucky. You're just in time for dinner."

"Dinner at 4:30?"

"We're having dinner early," he said. "Your luck" He handed me a big mug of coffee. I took a long, heavenly sip, set it down, and wrestled out of my last fleece layer. I was down to my base layer, a skin-tight black shirt and polypro tights. My knee braces were wrapped around the outside of my tights, and the chemical heat packs that I had stuffed inside my pants that morning had found their way inside the knee braces. My arms and legs looked like charred twigs. The warmer-stuffed neoprene braces made my knees look grotesquely deformed.

"Thank you so much," I said to the man. "I'm sorry. I know they told us your name at the race meeting ..."

"I'm Peter, and this is my wife, Tracy," he said, pointing to a kind-looking woman sitting next to Kathi.

"Wow," I said. "You guys are really kind to let us stay here. I mean, wow. I can't imagine what it would be like to roll into McGrath and just have nowhere to go."

"That's what it's like in Nome," Kathi said. "You get there too late at night, and you just have to hope there's a hotel open."

Nome is where she and Bill were still headed. The far-away town on Alaska's west coast was still 750 miles away. Where they sat in McGrath, they were less than one-third of the way through their race. All of the Iditarod Trail's biggest, hardest, most remote sections still lay ahead. Their race was a three-plus-week effort just to ride a bike to Nome, where no one would be waiting for them. I just smiled at Kathi with genuine astonishment, because I had ridden my bike to McGrath, and it was the hardest thing I had ever done, and I could not contemplate or understand the vastness of her goal.

Peter directed me to the table just as the rest of the strange crew was starting to gather ... Bill and Kathi, Peter and Tracy, the Italian cyclist, and another older Euro cyclist who said his name was Rok. I hadn't even washed my hands yet, let alone the rest of my body, covered as it was in six-day-old sweat and the stench of the ages. I was uncomfortably aware of the impropriety of my presence.

I considered asking to excuse myself from the table for a second to rinse my hands, but the thought of it seemed almost laughable. I had been eating out of a frozen feed bag for six days, scooping fragments of food out of the snow with my dirty mittens, and everyone knew it. The group didn't seem to mind anyway that I was dirty and addled and still struggling to bring my head back to the land of the living. They just laughed and chatted in four different languages and passed around gigantic bowls of food. I took a pork chop and a dollop of potatoes as Peter handed me a huge glass of orange juice. I picked around at my plate — how could I still not be hungry? — but decided to do the polite and smart thing and stuff it down.

After dinner, I gulped down the rest of my coffee and asked Tracy if I could go upstairs and take a shower. She handed me a towel and the package I had mailed to her house — a box containing clean street clothes. I pulled out my jeans and cotton T-shirt and saw the clothes Geoff had packed. Seeing his shirt and faded pair of corduroy pants made my heart sink, because Geoff wasn't there. And Geoff wasn't coming. Even as the satisfaction about finishing the race finally started to seep in, so did the sadness that Geoff couldn't be there himself, holding his own clean clothes, experiencing his own moment of sweeping relief.

I pulled out his shirt and decided I liked it better than the one I had packed. I walked into the bathroom and peeled off my last Iditarod layer. The shirt clung to my back like a scab, grabbing my skin as it ripped away. As my tights came off, I noticed dark red indentations in my legs where the seams had dug in. Those clothes had become a part of me, too, and with my base layer finally off, my transformation was complete.

I looked at my naked body in the mirror, unable to fully accept that the reflection staring back at me was mine. My ribs and collar bone protruded sharply out of my skin. My shoulders were knobby and thin. I wrapped my fingers around my abdomen and pulled away a surprising amount of loose skin. In the six-day-process of the race, with its unintentional starvation diet and dehydration, I had probably lost at least 10 pounds. But from my vantage point in the mirror, it looked and felt like 30. I was an emaciated skeleton. A translucent shell of what I used to be. I turned around. Sure enough, two crescent shaped, white and pink blisters had formed above each of my rear cheeks. Butt frostbite. It surely did exist.

I took no pleasure from the weight I had lost, because my body looked so battered and abused. The fact that I had done all of that to myself in the short span of six days was frightening, and I had to look away.

I walked to the shower and turned on the hot water. I expected to next several minutes to transport me to a heaven I had never before known. The best showers in my life always followed long, physical events. Washing away hard effort beneath a stream of hot, soapy water was a pleasure that could never be duplicated under normal circumstances. I figured the act of washing away six days, 350 snow miles and the horrible stench of the Farewell Burn would feel as wonderful as washing away the bulk of my life's sins. But as I stood beneath the showerhead and let the warm water caress my back, I only felt pain. Cringing pain, as hot water stung every sore and blister I had accumulated. I had to turn down the temperature. The pain subsided. A numbness settled in. It felt vaguely familiar. I grabbed the bar of soap and mindlessly went through a routine I had completed thousands of times back when I was still a real person.

I walked down the stairs wearing Geoff's T-shirt, a 2006 Little Su 50K race shirt. Both the shirt and my jeans were crumpled from spending several weeks stuffed in a postal box. My feet throbbed and my knees ached. I took careful steps so as to not appear like I was hobbling.

The temptation to limp was surprising. I had made it through the past six days moving and walking almost normally. Why would I stiffen up now? It was as though my body knew I was finished, and that it was no longer needed for survival, so the shutdown commenced. But just downstairs were Bill and Kathi and two Euro bikers who all had 750 more miles ahead of them. And even though all of my miles were behind me, I felt a strong urge to not appear broken — to appear as though, given the urge, I could just sit right back down on my bicycle and join them.

"So, do you feel better now?" Kathi asked as I settled into the plush couch with another cup of coffee.

"Much," I lied. I had a sinking suspicion that simple act of sitting down was going to be my last movement for the night. Only another significant effort was even going to get me back up those stairs. I really was broken, and I didn't understand. As horrible as I had felt at the end of other days during the race, I always had the confidence that I could wake up and do it again the next day. Why would my body fail on me now? Because it no longer mattered? The thought was disconcerting ... if my physical state was so close to shutdown, maybe it really was my broken spirit that kept me going all along.

I took a long swig of coffee and winced at its strange, salty taste. I decided it must have been an electrolyte imbalance — another physical failure I hadn't noticed before that moment. The maladies were quickly adding up. Weight loss, bruises, frostbite, nutritional deficiencies, blistered feet, sore knees, stiff muscles, numb fingers ... medically, I was a wreck. Kathi, on the other hand, looked like she was kicking back after a day on the beach.

"So," I said. "When are you and Bill heading out?"

"Probably the day after tomorrow," Kathi said. "We're hoping the Iditarod trail breakers will come through by then and put in the trail. They haven't been through yet, so all those guys that went ahead are probably all camped together, waiting for the snowmachines."

"How many guys went on to Nome?" I asked.

Kathi looked up like she was counting in her head. "Six so far," she said. "I think there were six."

"Pete was with them, wasn't he?"

Kathi smiled. "Yeah, Pete's going to Nome. It was supposed to be a big secret. Bill and I knew because we sent his drop bags."

"I suspected it," I said. "Now I guess I'm one of the last to know."

Pete's description of his 2007 race had been so ingrained in my mental landscape that I could almost see him out there, somewhere west of nowhere, pushing his bike over a trailless, blank expanse. It made me smile, and shudder.

"So what about you?" Kathi asked. "You've made it. You're looking pretty fresh. Are you going to stick around and go on to Nome with us?"

I laughed out loud. "Ha! No. You think I look fresh. But no, no, no, no, no. No Nome. No. I can't even begin to form a concept of what 18 more days of that would feel like.

"Hopefully it will be less than 18," Kathi said. "If we get a good trail."

"Do you feel like you're ready?" I asked.

She nodded. "Yeah. We feel really good. Excited. But we're still taking it one day at a time. We have to, if we want to make it."

I just shook my head. "I just can't imagine," I said. "And I've tried."

"Well, either way, you should come back next year," Kathi said. "Sounds like Geoff has already signed up."

"Now that I can imagine," I said. "He hates to be beaten by anything. I don't think you guys could keep him away from McGrath next year."

"He'll beat the record if he makes it," Kathi said. "Are you sad that you missed the record?"

"Your record?" I said. "No. Definitely not. I was never gunning for it. I don't think I would have made it out of Rohn if I was."

"Why's that?"

"Well, because I was running on fumes by Rohn," I said. "More than that, though, Rohn is where my perspective about this race completely changed. There's a lot more to this race than glory and goals. It's much deeper ... much more internal, don't you think?"

Kathi nodded. "It's really beautiful, too. That's why this race is so addicting."

"Addicting," I laughed. "That's what they tell me. "It's probably easier to believe after the hangover wears off."

"So will you be back?" Kathi asked.

"I couldn't say," I said. "Right now, I still just want to get through tomorrow."

Kathi smiled. "You'll be back."

She and I both knew it. "So, when does it end?" I asked.

"I don't know," she said. "Hopefully never."

I felt a strong connection to Kathi and wanted to reach out and hug her, but decided it would be best to restrain that emotion. My ongoing urges to sing or scream or break down and start bawling signaled a chemical imbalance that made me question everything I felt, even the warmth, love and satisfaction. So I held my silence. But I suspected Kathi understood my feelings, just the same.

I peeled myself away from the couch and managed to make it back upstairs to the computer room. I typed up a quick e-mail to the world before settling into the bed that Peter and Tracy had generously offered me. I felt a strangeness coursing through my body. It went beyond the stiff muscles and throbbing joints, beyond the bruises and swelling. It was a surreal sensation that cut straight through my heart.

I held my hand to my chest and pressed my fingers into my rib cage. My heart was still racing, but it felt like a quiet murmur against the palm of my hand. I laid down and stared at the ceiling, glowing gray in the moonlight. Sleep was as close as it had ever been, but I fought it with all the strength I had left. I knew that once I woke up again, everything about the race was going to be a dream, a memory, a piece of my past that no longer had an all-encompassing hold on me. I had worked so hard for that moment that I couldn't just let it slip away like that. I needed to know why I was there. I needed my extreme emotions and my murmuring heart and the moonlight over McGrath to tell me what it all meant.

"How am I different?" I thought. "How have I changed?"

The ghost of myself that still lurked beneath my battered body simply stirred from her six-day slumber and said, "you haven't."

I fell asleep to haunting thoughts of moments in my life that had come to define me ... Jill as scared little girl ... Jill as wanderer ... Jill as journalist ... Jill as adventurer ... Jill as cyclist ... Jill as strongwoman ... Jill and Geoff. I wondered how this moment would have played out differently if any one of my life's trails had led to a different destination. Or if it would have played out differently at all. Or if I was simply living a path that had been ingrained in my past and future, all along.

I had followed the ghost trail to McGrath, and what it had taught me was that I was little more than a ghost myself ... a traveler without a starting point or a destination, forever drifting between memories and the moment, forever cycling toward a nonexistent end.

Eastern Alaska
September 9, 2005

"Are you scared?" Geoff asked me as he tossed a stone into a cold, probably unnamed lake.

"A little," I said. "There are really a lot of unknowns. I mean, we haven't worked out much of this at all. Where we're going to live ... what you're going to do ... how we're going to move our cats, or if we can even find a place that allows cats. We're sort of just coming up here. I have that job offer, but just about nothing else."

"We'll figure it out," Geoff said.

A deep evening red spread across the clouds in the sky and reflected beside our feet as Geoff and I walked along the lake's shoreline. Hundreds of small fish — grayling, perhaps — leaped out of the still water in a feeding frenzy. We were somewhere just west of the Alaska-Yukon border, camping after another full day of driving toward Homer. The state park we had stopped at looked strangely familiar.

"Sometimes I just feel like I'm in this perpetual state of drift."

"I still have that place in Palmer," Geoff said. "If you're not dead-set on Homer, then we can go live there."

"I'd still rather go where I have a job," I said.

"Well then you're set," Geoff said.

"Maybe so," I said. "It's just that I'm ... tired of this, I guess."

"Tired of moving?"

"Tired of drifting. I had a good thing going in Idaho."

"Are you unhappy that you came?"

I looked out over the horizon, lined with spruce and sinking into deep shadow. "No. No, I'm not."

"It'll work out," Geoff said. "You always worry too much."

"Maybe so," I said.

I glanced back toward the campground. "We've been here before, haven't we?"

"I think so," Geoff said. "I think this is where we stayed with Chris and Jen our last night in Alaska. Well, before we headed back to the Yukon and down to Haines and Juneau and stuff."

"This is where we made the blueberry pie on the camp stove, isn't it?"

"Maybe. We made a few of those," Geoff said.

"Yeah, but I remember this place. You and Chris and Jen were all being lethargic, so I set out on this weird nature walk and ended up spending four hours picking blueberries. Remember the bags and bags I came back with? We made the pie, and even froze a bunch. We ended up taking some of them back to Utah."

"We were kind of lethargic a lot on that trip, weren't we?" Geoff said.

"Yeah," I said. "I was, too. If I had been smart, I would have actually trained for the bike tour. Instead, you know, I just got in shape on the trip. That worked out so well."

Geoff laughed. "Do you even ride your bike any more?"

"I think I went riding three, maybe four times the entire time I lived in Idaho," I said. "Went out a couple times on the farm roads. I went mountain biking once with that Gary Fisher you talked me into buying. I don't know ... there's good biking in Idaho. I just wasn't into it."

"Probably because you spent all of your time at the gym."

"Yeah," I said. "Pretty much my entire social network was shaped around the Apple Fitness and my job."

"So how to you plan to work out in Homer?"

"I don't know," I said. "I looked into it, and there's really not much in the way of gyms. I'll probably start riding my bike again to stay in shape. I've really been meaning to. It's kind of stupid, really, that I spent all of my free time in Idaho either with my friends, watching movies, or pedaling a spin bike at the gym."

"What about winter?"

"I don't know. Maybe I'll take up running."

"I need to start running again," Geoff said. "Dane got me into this habit of drinking a couple beers every night." He grabbed his stomach and pinched the fabric of his flannel shirt. "I bet I gained 10 pounds this summer."

"I don't think it's physically possible for you to gain 10 pounds," I said.

"Well, anyway, I'm going to start running again," Geoff said. "It's probably really easy to go crazy up here in the winter if you don't do something."

"I wonder what people up here really do all winter long," I said. "When it's so cold and dark. Really, they should have an Apple Fitness on every corner in Alaska."

"I remember they have coffee carts on every corner," Geoff said.

We walked back to our camp site. Geoff had erected his weather-worn tent next to my overstuffed car. My two bicycles, a creaky touring bike and a nearly new mountain bike, rested on the roof rack.

"I'm thinking I could buy one of those bike trainers and keep doing my spin routines during the winter," I said. "I've also read about these studded tires they make for bikes, so you can ride on icy roads in the winter."

"Why not just ski?" Geoff asked.

"Maybe I'll learn to do that, too," I said. "I still have a lot to learn about life in Alaska."

"It's not that much different," Geoff said.

I looked south over the lake, and beyond that, wilderness stretching all the way to the sea. "I think it really is," I said.

We crawled into the tent and settled in our sleeping bags. My 0-degree-rated bag still carried the sweet smell of wet sand and something vaguely smoky even though, before we started driving north, I hadn't used it in many months. We had one more day's drive to the Anchorage area to visit friends, and after that, we were just a few hours from home. Home. So far away from anywhere.

I pulled my bag up over my face and breathed in the nostalgic odor until it faded into a background of spruce-tinted air. I shivered a little, though the place wasn't cold. Was this really fear that I was feeling, or was it just some inherent sense of liberation? After all, the only thing I could count on now was change, and the only thing I needed to take care of was myself.

It was a happy problem to have — too many choices. But there were choices I had made, and choices I was going to have to make, and maybe even choices I would have no choice but to make. I had this anxious sense that I already had taken too many steps down a path that I would not be able to turn back. But, then again, every step is like that. There are an endless number of spur trails along the way, but at the end of it all, life only goes one direction.

"Geoff?" I said, as I pulled my bag back down from my face.

"Yeah?" he answered in a quiet voice that told me he was already nearly asleep.

"I love you," I said.

"Love you, too," he said groggily. I looked out of the vestibule at a wash of stars splattered across the sky and smiled, because it wasn't a bad place to be.

2008 Iditarod Trail Invitational

- Forty five competitors started the Iditarod Trail Invitational on Feb. 24, 2008. Twenty eight finished the race to McGrath. Thirteen racers went on to Nome. Of those, six finished.

- Jay Petervary won the race to McGrath with a time 3 days, 14 hours and 20 minutes, after a long, near-continuous push that took him all the way from Rohn to the finish. He continued on toward Nome but scratched in Nulato after pushing his bike through soft snow for several days.

- Pete Basinger finished the 2008 race in 10th place after breaking his pedal, twice, and becoming ill before Nikolai, which forced him to take a long layover. He finished the race to McGrath in 4 days, 2 hours and 27 minutes. He went on to Nome, traveling with Jay Petervary, Rocky Reifenstul and Carl Hutchings in a tight-knit group of four. All but Carl decided to quit in Nulato after the push had them moving as slowly as 30 miles per day. However, after Pete failed to secure a quick flight out of town, Carl talked him into rejoining the race. The two traveled together until Pete broke ahead near the end, finishing the race to Nome in 18 days, 4 hours and 33 minutes. Carl finished in second place with a time of 18 days, 12 hours and 30 minutes. Rok Kovak of Slovenia, who had at times been many days behind the leaders, timed his trip perfectly to hit the best conditions the Iditarod Trail had to offer in 2008. He finished the race to Nome in 18 days, 21 hours and 20 minutes.

- Kathi Hirzinger-Merchant and Bill Merchant finished the race to McGrath in 5 days, 9 hours. They waited several days in McGrath before moving on to Nome, finding much better riding conditions than the race leaders had dealt with. However, later in the race they encountered warm, soft conditions followed by extreme cold and driving wind. A complete white-out forced them to bivvy one night on the sea ice of the Norton Sound. They continued the steady push and completed their goal in 25 days, 12 hours and 58 minutes. Kathi was the first woman ever to ride a bike to Nome. Bill became the oldest man to do so.

- Antonio Frezza, the Italian cyclist, finished the race to McGrath in 5 days, 13 hours.

- Ann Ver Hoef was the leading foot competitor when she scratched from the race in Nikolai with mild frostbite on her eyes and face. She made a full recovery and swore months later that she would never attempt the Iditarod Trail Invitational again. As of this writing, she is listed on the 2009 roster.

- Geoff Roes scratched in Finger Lake after pressing on with swelling and severe pain in his ankle. He completed the first 135-mile section of the race faster than anyone has on foot. He is registered for the 2009 race.

- Jill Homer completed the race to McGrath in 6 days, 2 hours and 20 minutes, in 17th place. She has full intention of entering the 2009 race to mend her myriad of mistakes. This book is her coming-out celebration.

GHOST TRAILS

JILL HOMER grew up in Sandy, Utah, and spent many childhood vacations camping and hiking in the desert with her family. She graduated from the University of Utah in 2000 with a bachelor's degree in journalism. She moved to Alaska in September 2005 and took up endurance cycling as a way to stay fit and sane during the winter. She has tried her luck at a handful of races, including the Susitna 100, the 24 Hours of Kincaid, the Soggy Bottom 100, the 24 Hours of Light and the Iditarod Trail Invitational. She works as a newspaper editor and designer in Juneau, Alaska, where she lives with Geoff Roes and two cats. She keeps a blog of her adventures at **http://arcticglass.blogspot.com.**

GHOST TRAILS